Testify to the Light

The Spiritual Biography of Andy Gustafson

Blessings on your reading
and conversations.

Rev Dr Betsy Waters

Testify to the Light

The Spiritual Biography
of Andy Gustafson

BY

M. ELIZABETH WATERS

ZION PUBLISHING

Cover design by Mary Ylvisaker Nilsen
Cover Photography by June Cloutier

Unless otherwise noted, the photos are part of the Gustafson family collection. Pictures and public web postings are used with permission of the Gustafson family and the Massachusetts Conference of the United Church of Christ.

ISBN-13: 978-1517317850

ISBN-10: 1517317851

For discounted bulk orders, contact the author:
www.renewingchurches.com

Published by Zion Publishing
Des Moines IA

Preface

ANDY GUSTAFSON created a game he called Stump the Steward, designed to impress the interview committee of the Massachusetts Conference of the United Church of Christ. Following his first interview, the team debated whether this country lawyer was the right fit for the state-level minister of Stewardship and Finance, a position that required theological skill, personal connection, and knowledge of how to invite generous giving. Stump the Steward challenged participants to find a Bible text that was unrelated to stewardship, to throw at him the hardest passage they could imagine, a passage that Andy could not link to God's grace and power, a set of verses that was useless when integrating generosity into congregational life. Andy bubbled as he introduced the game, his commitment to spreading the Good News apparent to all present. The committee was delighted. This was exactly the kind of stewardship leadership they sought.

At Annual Meeting, the yearly gathering of all the United Church of Christ congregations in Massachusetts, Andy engaged delegates in the game, daring them to find a text too obtuse to use, fielding passages from Job and Kings with aplomb, giddy as he linked bloody battles and frenzied mobs to God's grace, adeptly turning conversations about money into joyful play. In the following months, Andy brought the game to local churches, his large frame scrunched into metal folding chairs, his affable smile engaging cranky trustees, his keen intellect connecting text and life, his deep faith reframing fear about deficit budgets into opportunities for gratitude, into joyful thanksgiving that spilled out into the whole congregation.

But at heart, Andy's life was the real masterpiece of Stump the Steward, his personal tragedy providing the greatest challenge to be thrown at him, his life experience testifying to how within even the most horrific set of events, God is present. He chose to live again, to find joy again, to embody the text, "The Light shines in the darkness and the darkness will not overcome it"—that was Andy's most amazing act, the most profound linking of text and grace. Andy blessed the world. He was the unstumpable steward, the humble soul, a spiritual giant, and a lover of God.

Let me introduce myself as well. I am Betsy Waters, an ordained pastor, serving as an intentional interim minister in the Massachusetts Conference of the United Church of Christ. I heard about Andy from a friend who sat on that interview committee and who was involved in stewardship efforts in the conference. That was in 2004. I listened to Andy speak at various meetings and resonated with his approach to stewardship. I invited him to work with each of the three churches I pastored over the decade of his service, and tried out his small learning group focused on generosity. I traveled to New Orleans with him and another person, building a partnership focused on rebuilding following Hurricane Katrina, a mission we both treasured. I liked him, but I confess I found him more socially clumsy than impressive. He was very attentive and genuine, but not as articulate and polished as I expected of the state-level staff of my church. He was more a storyteller than a teacher.

It was my short time as a temporary minister at Andy's church that took our relationship deeper. At a visit soon after he was diagnosed with cancer, I asked him about his relationship with God. Andy replied, "I know God is with me. It's hard to explain exactly." He paused and looked at me, adding, "But you get that, Betsy." Those words continue to resonate, to lead me, to challenge me to find the words to testify to that Presence, to that Light. I was blessed to pastor Andy and his church, to accompany him and his family in his last months on earth, to be the officiant at the celebration of his life, to be entrusted with telling his story and the story of his community of faith.

Although in writing this book I have striven to be thorough in my research, interviewing many people, perusing photos and clippings, searching for news articles, and tapping my own experience, I have also used my imagination. Though I have never altered the basic facts of the story as I learned them, I have sometimes embellished a bit upon what I could document was said, heard, seen, or thought. For example, I do not know actually what happened in the grief support group Andy attended, so I created a leader and a structure common among such support groups and populated the group with members who might have attended. All the stories Andy tells in this section are true, but I do not know whether he told them in this context.

Andy's spiritual journey was a paradox, simultaneously ordinary and extraordinary, both incredibly painful and overflowing with joy, a combination of awkwardness and authenticity, at one moment restrained and another boisterous. I hope that sharing Andy's uniquely inspiring story might be a launching pad for others to share their own faith journey. To that end, there is a set of appendices to provide a format and questions for three different six-to-eight session studies: one on spiritual journey, one focused on grief, and a third on specific topics. In addition, there is a plan for a stewardship event that draws on this book.

If you wish to contact the author, a link can be found on the website www.renewingchurches.com.

May you be blessed in your reading and conversation.

Foreword and Gratitude

Thank you. A book like this does not come together without a community of people and a cloud of witnesses. I step out with some trepidation, knowing that I will probably omit many others who deserve thanks and recognition.

I thank Carole Gustafson for trusting me to share Andy's and her story and allowing me to write this biography. I am grateful for the people who offered their remembrances in words and in print. Knowing there is a risk of omitting people, I still want to thank Karen and Shelley Gustafson, Christine and Beth Morgan, Bill May, Peter Wells, Don Remick, Jim Antal, Mark Seifried, Rufus Cushman, Dick Sparrow, Gail Kendricks, Stephen Hemmen, Victoria Gaisford, and Liz Magill.

I used many articles from the *Boston Globe,* particularly ones from December 1987 to October 1988. I reviewed newsletters from the Townsend Congregational Church, materials from the Massachusetts Conference United Church of Christ (MACUCC) website, postings from Facebook and Ancestry, and the book *Once Upon a Crisis* by Bill May. I also drew extensively on my own experience.

I want to thank those who helped with the writing. Collegeville Institute's course "Words That Sing," taught by Mary Nilsen, awakened in me the desire to write, and the belief that I had something to say I thank the readers who gave me feedback: Kim Woosley, Linda Johnson, Shantia Wright-Gray, Jane Willan, Wade Heimer, the Cape Cod book group and Jerry Rardin. I appreciate the hard work and love showered by my editors, Sue Rardin, Jane Rowe, and Mary Nilsen.

And thank you to all who cheered and supported this journey.

Contents

To Avari Rose
and any future grandchildren of Andy,
so you may know the story of
your inspiring grandfather

The Apocalypse

Fog cloaked the gully on Saunders Road the first morning of December 1987, the Tuesday after Thanksgiving, as the Gustafson family gathered for breakfast. With a playful tone, Andy prompted his five-year-old son Billy to instruct his teddy bear to sit properly at the table. Billy responded proudly, "See, bear, this is how to sit." Andy poured milk on the three cereal bowls.

Cilla set out buttered toast, served juice to the children, poured coffee for herself and her husband, but did not sit down. Instead, she unearthed the first box of Christmas decorations, holding up some of the family favorites. "I love that one," Abby exclaimed. "December is my favorite month." Almost eight, she chattered about plans for her birthday, a slumber party proposed for the next weekend, her second-grade classmates already as excited as she was at the prospect. She loved school, and insisted this day on wearing the blue and white Spaulding Memorial elementary school t-shirt.

Cilla and Billy giggled about teddy bear day at their school, the Townsend Cooperative Play School. Cilla taught the three year olds while Billy attended the four-year-old group. Knowing his class would read the book *Corduroy,* one of his favorites, Billy dressed in the green Oshkosh overalls that matched his teddy's outfit even though it would be an hour before mother and son left the house.

Andy's thoughts focused on today's meeting with his real estate partner. He worried about yet another glitch, but hoped that the foreclosure on the hotel would finally, finally come together. Nevertheless, he enjoyed the family's parting routine: he hugged and kissed his children, tousling Billy's hair. He kissed and hugged Cilla, then put on his black overcoat and hat, grabbed his briefcase, the first out the door, calling back, "I love you," which all three echoed in turn. It would be a memory he would replay for years to come, but in this moment, he shifted his focus toward work.

The day proceeded as usual. Abby boarded the bus to school near the end of her driveway. Billy and Cilla drove to the preschool located at the Congregational Church and Andy met clients in his small office in the center of town.

Andy's Townsend, Massachusetts' law practice, more financially fragile than he had imagined, relied increasingly on the retainer of a speculative real estate broker. The broker, keenly aware of upcoming foreclosures, had suggested a partnership. Together, they would buy, refurbish, and manage a hotel in Gardner, with Andy taking on additional responsibilities and receiving a significant boost in income. The first hurdle in the legal process had unearthed a tangle of creditors, with multiple liens, unpaid back taxes, and clouded ownership. Many parties needed to agree to the terms, signing off their rights at less than 100% of indebtedness. The original deadline of early November had come and gone without a deal. Both Andy and his partner had to convince unhappy creditors of the reasonableness of the settlement. The tedious and tenuous business deal drew deeply on Andy's negotiation skills.

But that day, December 1, 1987, the agreement came together. All parties signed. They owned a hotel. Andy, overjoyed, called home in the late afternoon to give Cilla time to arrange for a sitter, so they could go out to celebrate. No one answered the phone. He tried two more times in the next hour to no avail.

Puzzled, Andy remembered that many Tuesdays, Cilla's sister Christine and the cousins came to visit. The sisters might have taken the children out to play and would probably be home when he got there, he thought to himself. He finished the last details at the office, stuffed his briefcase quickly, and, bubbling with exhilaration tinged just slightly with uncertainty, drove the ten minutes across town. Turning the corner of the quiet dead-end street, taking his long driveway by the wooded gully toward the house on the knoll, catching sight of Cilla's maroon van in the driveway, and noticing the house without lights in the late autumn darkness, he wrinkled his brow. Yet with such good news to share, he continued with a light step into the house, throwing open the front door, and calling out, "Cilla, are you home?" No answer. He picked up the phone to call the family's babysitter for information. Perhaps she would know why the car would end up in the driveway when Cilla and the children were not home. "I don't know," came the reply.

Uneasy, but still believing there would be an explanation, he bounded up the stairs to exchange his suit for more relaxed wear for the planned evening of fun. He called out again, anticipating the surprise, flung open the bedroom door and froze. Cilla's scantily clothed body sprawled face down on the bed, her skin ashen, her arms and legs spread eagle, tied to the bed. For one moment, time stopped. Then Andy stumbled down the stairs to the kitchen. Shaking, his vision blurred by tears, he struggled to dial 911. His cry for help was punctuated by shrieks and moans that made his message almost incomprehensible. Next, he phoned his parents, sharing only a few words. He felt compelled to go upstairs again. It was then he noticed the two bullet holes in the pillowcase and looked no further. He staggered back to the kitchen, pacing, kicking cabinets, and repeating, "My wife is dead." "My wife is dead." He didn't, he couldn't look for the children.

Cilla, that was Andy's pet name for Priscilla. How he loved her! She was his one and only, and they were smitten with each other, bonded so deeply they were almost one person. Cilla had been about eleven when she moved to his hometown of West Brookfield, Massachusetts, the oldest daughter of the new pastor of their church—not that his family attended very often. Andy, a bit of a late bloomer in junior high, focused on Boy Scouts and didn't participate in the church youth group. By contrast, the church was the center of Cilla's life. She was part of the ministry team: singing in the choir, reading scripture in front of the sanctuary, waitressing at the church suppers, and providing leadership at the youth group. In these roles, she exuded competence and maturity.

When Andy finally began to notice girls in high school, it was Cilla, with the surprising combination of a bubbly personality and a quiet kindness, who caught his eye. When his attempts to get her to notice him at school failed, he decided to go to church. That will make an impression, he thought to himself. Selecting his best outfit, pulling his long blond hair into a pony tail, borrowing the family car and arriving for worship ten minutes early, he sat expectantly in a side pew. She didn't come over. At coffee hour after church, he loaded his plate with goodies and followed her around, telling jokes and laughing before completing the punch lines. She stopped once or twice to listened politely, but then turned to converse with other parishioners. He remembered his discouragement. Later he heard how Cilla's younger sisters giggled about this geeky suitor and teased Cilla mercilessly. Nah, Andy's too goofy, Cilla complained to herself, shaking her head.

After high school, Andy commuted to Worcester State College, and a year later Cilla followed. She found freshman year in college to be lonely and disorienting, a much harder adjustment than she had expected. Perhaps that is why, when she ran into Andy, now a sophomore, she greeted him with a smile and lingered to hear some corny jokes. Although still unsure of himself around girls, particularly this young woman, Andy recalled the loneliness of his own first semester and assumed she needed a friend. He watched her relax, smile, and open up as they would stop to chat on campus. Maybe, he thought to himself, maybe this time she will be more interested in me. A couple of weeks into that first semester, he spotted Cilla sitting alone in the cafeteria. After carrying his tray to her table piled high with plates and glasses, he unloaded the spread across from her, catching the milk teetering seconds before it would have spilled. He mumbled, "Umm - I'm glad I found you."

Cilla brightened, "Me too." She chattered about her day as Andy almost inhaled his meal, taking big bites, gulping his milk, and trying to relax.

Soon, Andy and Cilla commuted together back and forth to school, talking about history class, current events, and school activities. One night coming home from Worcester somewhat later than usual, sitting in the car in her driveway, the night sky particularly brilliant, the topic shifted to astronomy. Andy slipped his arm around Cilla's shoulders, directing her eyes to the sky. "That line of stars helps locate the constellation Orion. And see there, the Big Dipper. You follow those two stars to find the little dipper and then the North Star."

They both remembered that first kiss. Soon they were more than conversation partners, they were smitten with each other.

Priscilla and Andy Gustafson
about 1978

They planned and dreamed a life. They expected to have a family and grow old together. And now, in her early thirties, his wife had been tortured and shot. She was dead.

Accused

Patrolman John Johns arrived minutes after the 911 call. Finding Andy beside himself with anguish, he focused on calming him down. When Sergeant Irving Marshall arrived, Patrolman Johns left the kitchen to search the house, room-by-room, closet-by-closet. In a short time, he returned, his face white and his hands shaking. Finding Andy pacing and crying, the officer asked him to sit. Johns took a deep breath, put his arm on Andy's shoulder and whispered with tears in his eyes, "We found the children. They are dead." Andy collapsed onto the table, wailing as if his soul had been ripped from his body.

When Police Chief Bill May arrived, Marshall took him outside to bring him up to date. May took charge of the investigation, knowing that because family members are the perpetrators in three out of four cases of violence in the home, Andy was the prime suspect. It didn't matter that he was the town's lawyer, a church member, or a volunteer for local causes. May must interrogate him now, on the scene, before evidence could be lost. After securing the premises, May instructed an officer to put Andy in the back seat of the cruiser and drive him to the end of the driveway. Andy huddled in the back seat, behind the barred divider, alone in the cold, dark December evening, accused of the unthinkable crime. He clutched himself and sobbed.

May walked through the house, speaking with each of his officers, reviewing procedures. He called the state police and the district attorney's office. Then he walked to the cruiser at the end of the driveway, instructing Andy to step outside the vehicle. He asked question after question, often repeating what Andy said, asking for clarification because Andy could hardly speak. Andy's parents arrived to offer support, ultimately standing, one on each side, steadying their son's big frame, now wilted like a frostbit flower, as he mumbled monosyllabic replies. May observed the details of Andy's dress and demeanor. He wore his business suit, tie, and topcoat that was neither wet nor soiled. Physically, Andy could barely stand, his body limp and uncoordinated, his face gray, his eyes hollow. He was, as May reported later, like a dead man walking, a totally shattered human being.

Near the end of the interrogation, a family friend, having heard of the multiple police cars swarming around the Gustafsons' home, arrived to offer help. Andy, crying, gestured toward the house and shook his head. Chief May agreed that the friend could identify the children rather than asking Andy to do it.

May released Andy into the custody of his parents who took him to their home in West Brookfield. May called Middlesex County's Assistant District Attorney Tom Reilly, reporting that there was no physical evidence linking the husband to the crime, and by observation, his grief was too real, too pervasive, too devastating, in fact, so total as to make it seem impossible for him to have been the perpetrator. Andrew Gustafson was not a suspect, he concluded.

Andy left without seeing the children––Billy drowned in the upstairs bathtub, Abby's body found in four inches of water in the downstairs tub. Both had deep bruising around their necks, the injuries inflicted by someone taller and heavier than they. The friend provided the identification for the police records, an act that Andy deeply appreciated to the end of his life.

On the drive to West Brookfield, Andy was not alone in the back seat of the car. As his father drove, his mother cradled his head in her lap, both of them crying tears they did not think would ever end. They drove through the rural countryside, past barren trees and wind-swept leaves, with only a few houses now lighted for the season. Even the evergreen on the triangular common in West Brookfield was dark, as the lighting ceremony was days ahead.

They arrived at the family home of Leonard and Shirley Gustafson, where Andy had lived growing up. Here, he had shared dinners with his parents, an older brother and sister. Here, he had greeted his cousins for family reunions. Now, he and his parents began to make the phone calls to extended family to share this awful news. Soon, the family that had grown up in this house gathered again, having driven the hour or more in the late evening. They did not leave Andy alone through that long night.

The murder of one's whole family, is this not a kind of personal apocalypse, the end of a known world? It is our greatest fear. It signals the death and destruction of all that is beloved, of all sense of safety, of a predictable world, of meaning and purpose for living. It cuts the flow of time. It overwhelms our resources. It destroys the foundation of our life. It drowns us in a sea of despair.

Andy's world was smashed. How could anyone survive the murders of his wife and two children? And yet he did. He not only survived, but ultimately thrived, with joy and purpose in living. I got to know Andy as a funny, clumsy, spiritually insightful conference leader. I had heard hints of a tragedy, but did not learn the story fully until I became Andy's pastor in the last year of his life.

What supports a person to move from death to life, as Andy did, I wondered. As he and I met regularly during his final illness, he told stories that provided insight, and as we prepared his funeral, others contributed their perspectives. I came to realize that many people held the same question I did, that Carole, his second wife, wanted that story to be told, and that I felt called to be the storyteller. This was a spiritual journey the world needed to hear. In the tradition of testimony, I will continue to describe what happened as I understand it, interpreting those events, linking text and his life, demonstrating the way the Light shines in the darkness.

I note that apocalypse not only means a catastrophic disaster, but also, when translated literally from the Greek, means an unveiling, a revelation, particularly of the Good News that good overcomes evil. The core testimony and faith claim of the Christian faith is that we are an Easter People, that love is stronger than death, that hope triumphs, that life can emerge from the tomb. But these faith claims can seem abstract, just part of a story we learned in Sunday School, and not very relevant or powerful for today's living. My hope is that exploring Andy's life story will give the reader opportunities not only to connect Andy's life to the Easter story, but also to throw light on how the story is alive in the reader's world as well.

The First Hours

Back in Townsend, Police Chief May sought reinforcements from the state police. By 7:00 p.m., the two-story home swarmed with state troopers, another group fanned out to knock on doors, and a third unit stopped motorists on Route 119. "Did you see anything?" they repeatedly queried. The unexpected traffic jam, with whirring blue lights and uniformed officers, as well as state troopers ringing door bells and knocking loudly on front doors, detonated anxiety and then alarm, setting off a cascade of phone calls repeating whatever news each neighbor had, fueling the fear that a killer roamed free, randomly killing women and children.

Who might be next? How can this be happening here, in a community that feels so set apart from the turmoil of urban life? With contagious terror, doors were locked, guns emerged from hiding places, and parents held children close.

By 8:00 p.m. the district attorney's office issued a press release. A young teacher and her two children had been found dead in their home in the small town of Townsend, Massachusetts, just over the border from New Hampshire. The unreleased details spread quickly by word of mouth, neighbor to neighbor, the way they do in small towns: Priscilla Gustafson, the preschool teacher, had been shot, and her children strangled and drowned in their bathtubs. The elementary school principal, Anthony Luzzetti, activated the staff telephone tree, sharing the news that was known.

One of their students had been murdered, along with her family. Come to an emergency meeting before school tomorrow morning, the message concluded.

By 9:00 p.m. investigators had catalogued clues from inside the house, dogs had searched the outside perimeter, and troopers had gathered pieces of information, like puzzle pieces: interviews with dozens of neighbors, both adults and children, photos and measurements from the bedroom and bathrooms, some random hairs and fingerprints, a Converse sneaker footprint in the flower bed. With Andy eliminated as a suspect, the team urgently asked, "Who could have done such a crime?"

The homicide detectives met with police in Townsend and nearby villages to identify local suspects with similar MOs. Townsend officers mentioned a teen, Daniel LaPlante, who had been in and out of juvenile facilities. LaPlante, presently charged with a home invasion that included torturing the resident family, was out on bail pending that trial. The investigator put him on a short list for further investigation and continued to review other possible suspects. Before midnight, the homicide team had developed a list of five people of interest to be interviewed. That would be a task for tomorrow morning.

In West Brookfield, Andy could not sleep. He and his brother walked to the Boy Scout campsite behind their house, to the nearby cluster of Adirondack shelters and fire pits that had been so central in their growing-up years. They built a fire, sat together staring into the flames, mostly in silence, sometimes crying, sometimes sharing words. Finally, they acknowledged they were too cold to stay, put out the fire, walked home to toss fitfully on their beds for the rest of the night.

With daylight on Wednesday, the homicide team assigned tasks to the day shift, a large contingent of law enforcement officers. Assignments included five teams interviewing suspects, the dog unit investigating the trail in the woods, and patrol officers dispatched to be a visible presence all over town.

By 7:30 a.m., the staff of the Spaulding Memorial School assembled in the cafeteria, some with puffy eyes, some hugging each other, some crying softly. Many here knew the bright and charming Abby Gustafson, or had loved Cilla as the preschool teacher of their own children. The superintendent of schools and a bevy of professionals from other schools gathered in one corner of the room, sipping coffee prepared by the lunchroom staff. Luzetti circulated among his teachers, touching shoulders, hugging some, shaking his head as he listened. Then, the Superintendent went to the microphone. "Can we come together," he began. "What a tragic loss! Scary. I want everyone to know the news."

He reiterated the content of the news release and an update from Chief May, answering questions from the floor as best he could. "Someone will be talking with the Gustafsons, and we will pass that information along to you as we receive it. Last night, I called superintendents in neighboring towns, and they have responded by sending counselors, substitute teachers, and extra hands. The police department will have a car with two officers in our parking lot today. I want you to know there is a wide circle of support for all of you, for all of us, for the children and the families." He turned the microphone over to principal Luzetti.

"This is appalling and overwhelming news. It is hard to know quite what to do, but we do have an emergency plan we are following. I want to thank the custodial staff for setting up many private areas for counselors who can talk with staff or children. Anyone too distressed to work can take a break or leave. Notify the office to request a substitute. We will have teams prepared to come to your classroom to share the news, answer questions, and do a grief activity with the children. We have prepared a written statement for you to read to your class when you start the day, until the team gets to your classroom." Papers passed from hand to hand. "The statement contains the basic information, tells the children it is normal to cry or feel afraid, and that someone can talk with them if they ask.

"I imagine many families will keep their children home today," Luzetti continued. "So, we know this support will need to continue for a while. Our answering machines have many offers from local agencies and other school districts. We will arrange significant support for at least a week."

A tragedy like this reverberates. The school community grieves the loss of the child they knew. What does a teacher say to the second-grade classmates of Abby, to the children who rode the bus with her yesterday, to the questions raised by young and old? Then there is the terror of the moment, the unmediated fears. Who did this? Am I going to be killed when I go home from school? Is my mother going to die while I am away? Later, the questions about death and about why this happened would have more force. Now shock engulfed them like a shroud blocking all light.

It wasn't just the school. The whole town was reeling. At workplaces and coffee shops, at the grocery store and gas stations, people expressed their shock and their fear. To make matters worse, the media, drawn to the sensational story, posted television camera trucks around Townsend, eager to interview anyone with a new angle on the story. They took video of familiar landmarks and captured quotes from neighbors. The laments of the secretary of the board of selectmen flashed on screens across the country: "This is not supposed to happen in this kind of town. People are crushed, scared, and trying to figure out a way to deal with it."[1]

Many teams of law enforcement officers worked together. The canine team returned to Saunders Road, searched around the house, and followed a trail into the woods. They collected more evidence to give the detectives in a matter of hours. Teams of state troopers dispersed to interview the five people of interest identi-fied by investigators the previous evening. State Trooper Stephen Matthews and his partner would interview teen suspect Daniel LaPlante, who lived on the rural road just off Route 119. They drove to his house, found no one home, and waited in the drive-way.

In West Brookfield, Andy was numb with shock and exhaus-tion. When he could think at all, his mind flooded with memo-ries, with what if's, with questions of whether to continue to live. He remembered that Cilla would have reached out to God and had taught him how to bring his trials to Jesus. They had prayed together at night regularly and returned to prayer when things where difficult in their lives. She had guided him to repeat a verse or a passage over and over in his mind, as a way to be with God, especially when other ways were confounding. He tried to con-nect with the Holy, repeating familiar texts to himself, particularly Psalm 23:

The Lord is my shepherd, I shall not want.
He makes me lie down in green pastures;
he leads me beside still waters;
he restores my soul.
He leads me in right paths
for his name's sake.
Even though I walk through the darkest valley,
I fear no evil; for you are with me;
your rod and your staff—they comfort me.
You prepare a table before me
in the presence of my enemies;
you anoint my head with oil;
my cup overflows.
Surely goodness and mercy shall follow me
all the days of my life,
and I shall dwell in the house of the Lord
my whole life long. (NRSV)

But then he would stop and argue with himself. What kind of God could have allowed this violence? If there was a God, even. Could he believe naively, in the face of this horror? It was as if the campfire of his faith had been drenched and almost extinguished—but somehow embers remained. He kept returning to the spiritual practices he shared with Cilla, even though his shock, pain, and disbelief were overwhelming.

Operating almost on automatic pilot, he talked briefly by phone with the funeral home and his pastor, the Rev. Neil Lund. This brought little comfort, but they discussed options. Would they hold a funeral sooner or a memorial service later? He arranged a meeting with the funeral home and the pastor the next day. He talked with friends in Townsend, who offered to host a lunch for Andy's family following those appointments. He would meet with Cilla's family there.

The Suspect

The team of plainclothes state troopers, assigned to interview teen Daniel LaPlante, sat in the driveway of his home for more than an hour until a car drove in. Trooper Matthews and his partner approached twenty-year old Stephen LaPlante, who had just returned from his college class. Stephen allowed the officers to search his car and answered their questions. He told them that his brother Danny was likely at the library, at a tutoring session; this alternative to attending the high school had been arranged when he was released on bail.

The troopers drove across town to the library. Matthews spotted the tutoring pair, the youth slouched at the table until he recognized that the two strangers were coming to speak to him. "Hey, I'm not a bad guy!" Daniel bellowed for all to hear, his hands raised.

"Shh!" Matthews began, introducing himself and making certain he was talking to Daniel LaPlante. "I just have a few questions for you. You know the drill." Matthews spoke while his partner recorded the answers. "Where were you yesterday, December first?"

"At home, hanging out, watching TV." Daniel looked away from the officers. "Then I went with my mom to my niece's birthday party in Fitchburg."

"What did you wear yesterday?"

"I don't know. I guess gray sweat pants, a football shirt, and sneakers, like I always do."

"Like those?" Matthew pointed to the Converse sneakers on his feet.

"Yeah."

"When did you learn about the murders?" Matthews continued.

"Last night. It was on the news. I think it was eleven. My parents had the Boston channel on. We all heard it together. My dad and I looked up Saunders Road on the map."

Matthews gave instructions. "Please stay around town for the next couple of days. Remember, you are on bail."

"Yes, sir." He saluted in a flippant manner.

Late that morning, a group of town workers set up microphones on the Townsend Town Hall steps, attracting reporters like insects to a light. At midday, Middlesex County District Attorney Scott Harshbarger stood before a small crowd, cameras rolling, reviewing the known details and pleading, "At this point any information we can get is crucial."

Neighbors echoed dismay and dread across fences and by phone, trying to keep everyone safe. When Carole Seaver, a young widow who belonged to Andy's and Cilla's church, arrived home from Florida, she almost immediately received a call from another church member sharing the news of the murders and instructing her to lock doors and windows "because who knows who could be next." It was as if the serenity and safety of the whole world had been shattered.

At the LaPlante house, Stephen, joined by his buddy Michael, hung out, smoked a little weed, watched some TV, and kibitzed about the rumors they had heard about the murders.

Soon after noon, the screen door slammed, announcing Daniel's return from tutoring. Stephen, remembering the two times his brother had been accused of major crimes, chided him. "Some officers came by to ask you questions. I think it's about those murders. You better not have done it! Mom's risked the whole house to bail you out, to give you one last chance. She's done everything for you. You better not have messed up again." [2]

"Not me. Everyone always thinks it's me." He went to the kitchen to make a sandwich and came back to the living room to crash on the couch. Not long after, they heard a car drive in. Daniel must have caught a glimpse of the cruiser. "Cops!" he yelled, and hightailed it off the back porch before the troopers made it to the front door.

Stephen and his friend Michael showed the officers where Daniel had disappeared into the underbrush, but the foot officers found nothing during their initial search. They called for reinforcements and a manhunt began.

In minutes, multiple blue lights bounced off the houses and trees of West Elm Street as troopers and local police pursued the youth in the underbrush, but Daniel had an advantage. This terrain was like a second home for him. He had played here since he was a boy, had slept outside when home fights grew too heated, had created secret places to smoke weed and stash drugs, had developed routes through the trees guided only by familiar landmarks and outcroppings.

More officers knocked on the door of the 22 West Elm Street home, intent on executing a search warrant of the LaPlante house, where seventeen-year-old Danny lived with his mother, his stepfather, and his two brothers, one older and one younger. In Danny's room and elsewhere in the house, the search uncovered objects that people had reported missing in a series of break-ins in the last six weeks. The Gustafsons had been one of the families reporting such a robbery, noting the loss of a Statue of Liberty coin box containing a collection of Liberty silver dollars. The investigators found it, an easily identifiable object, in the search, along with other items that were probably stolen. The officers interviewed his brother Stephen and friend Michael. Their answers led the police to locate some .22 caliber ammunition in the house.

With the accumulation of evidence focused on Daniel and little pointing toward the other people of interest, law enforcement officers decided to make the manhunt public, both to seek help and to warn people of the danger. They knew it would increase the tension and fear in the community, but they needed to find this teen as soon as possible, for he could act again. Someone called the Gustafsons to alert them to the identification of a suspect, the fact that he had eluded capture, and the plan to make a public announcement. The family reeled in shock. A teenager from Townsend? How could this be?

The state police held a press conference that was broadcast as breaking news flashes on TVs across New England and rebroadcast as headlines across the country. A local young man, Daniel LaPlante, had been identified as the prime suspect: a white seventeen-year-old male, 5 feet 8 inches, 135 pounds, brown hair and brown eyes. He had evaded the police and was on the run. He should be considered armed and dangerous. The police pleaded for the public to come forward with any information. A hotline phone number flashed on the bottom of screens, and appeared in bold print on the fliers handed out and published in local papers. They reminded people to be extremely careful as they moved around town and to keep their children indoors.

More police descended on Townsend, searching the woods around West Elm Street, producing a cacophony of sound. Helicopters swooped low, the engines roaring, the rhythmic whoop of their blades threatening safety. Several canine teams swept the thick underbrush, searching for the smell, barking their presence. Police talked to each other and any in the woods, in shouts and bullhorns. The sounds echoed in people's bones, building fear and foreboding. Families hid in their locked houses, protecting loved ones from the cloud of danger and terror as best they could, as the December twilight faded into cold darkness. A killer was on the loose.

Wednesday night, with police lights flashing at roadblocks and sirens wailing in the distance, almost no civilian cars drove down streets. Everyone huddled in their own homes. Some families tried distraction, tried to laugh at TV comedies. Some cried together and wondered if the world was ending. Some brought guns or knives out of hiding places, keeping weapons near at hand, just in case. Others did what they rarely did—they prayed together for protection, for the capture of LaPlante, for the healing of all the families. Some chanted Psalm 23, not sure what else to do to keep themselves calm, while others drank more than the usual amount of alcohol to dull the terror. With doors and windows bolted, families slept together in one room, creating what safety they could.

Young LaPlante, so at home in the local woods, hid in dense underbrush, using tree branches to protect himself from the drizzle, traveling in fits and starts, crossing the line into the next town of Pepperell. It was a long night for LaPlante, for law enforcement, and for the local residents.

Thursday morning, parents drove children to school rather than have them wait for the bus, if they allowed them to go to school at all. The students at the secondary school pulsed with anxiety. They knew Danny LaPlante. He had a reputation as a scary, unpredictable kid. He often wore heavy-metal-band Iron Maiden t-shirts with gruesome images. Some of his classmates related a memory of a verbal altercation between two students, one student bullying another. Danny bolted from the opposite side of the playground, elbowed his way through the circle of students watching this fight, took hold of one of the boys involved in the argument and broke his arm. No warning. No explanation. No remorse. It was as though he thrived on hurting people. Those who remembered shuddered now.

All over the school, in classrooms and in halls, students whispered to each other—the cops haven't found him. They discovered that the middle-school gym had become a staging area for the FBI. Because of the possibility that LaPlante could cross state boundaries, the national agency and some New Hampshire State Police joined the search. The investigators interviewed staff and students to gain insight into LaPlante's patterns and interests. The whole scene was surreal. This happened in movies, not in little Townsend.

Even more television crews and print-media reporters invaded the town, some in their marked TV trucks, others in unmarked cars. Reporters pulled out their microphones and notepads whenever they saw people on the street, and would approach shoppers in grocery store parking lots and gas stations, throwing questions at them from a distance if they weren't allowed to get closer. The reporters gathered background on the town, the Gustafsons and the LaPlantes. There were ordinary stories about Danny, such as incidents during games on the soccer field. Some people talked about how smart he was, but how he seemed to turn his smarts in the wrong direction. A couple of people related stories of hearing Danny's mother yell at him, belittling him with put-downs, threatening him with punishments, calling him names. Others told anecdotes of listening to his mother defend her son's actions to the principal, aiming to make Danny the victim of school discipline.

One interviewee remembered another murder on that same street fifteen years before, another young teacher she thought. That murder had never been solved. Did they have a serial murderer? Logic said that the other killer couldn't be Danny, because he was too young. Could they be seeking the wrong person? Or could the murderer have been Danny's now-incarcerated father? Or was this street jinxed? It was scary to even think these questions.

The pastor of the church, the Rev. Lund, talked with reporters, giving background on the Gustafson family, talking about their involvement in church, and describing the children. "They weren't your average nice people. They were role models. That's what makes this so hard." Media broadcasts began with the Lund interview on the front steps of the church, but then panned out to images across town—the green with the gazebo, the schools and playgrounds, the ice cream shops and waterfront—as the reporter updated the story. The reporting, the intense manhunt, the revelations about people's lives, violated the norms of privacy in this New England town, undermining their rural identity.

Under the Shadow
of Terror

Thursday morning, several family members joined Andy for two appointments in Townsend, one with the funeral director and the other with Pastor Lund. The ongoing manhunt for Daniel LaPlante compounded the tragedy and amplified anxiety, yet their focus was how to celebrate the lives of Cilla, Abby, and Billy.

The family had been wrestling with questions of timing. If they chose a funeral, with the caskets present, it needed to be soon. A memorial service could happen later. Did they want to wait until the

Abby and Billy Gustafson,
circa 1986

police caught LaPlante? "I will not cede any more power to that young man. He will not control us," Andy asserted. They decided on a funeral at the church, regardless of what was happening in the search for the killer. Andy needed God's Light to shine in the darkness; he intended to focus attention on love rather than fear. The service would be Saturday morning, with cremation and burial to happen later. Under the circumstances, there would be no wake before the service or collation afterward. Andy could not tolerate a social time of greeting. The family would gather privately, in the home of friends.

They finished with the funeral home details and, rather than move to the church, they remained at the funeral home where Pastor Lund joined them. Lund introduced himself, learned the names of those gathered, and offered a prayer. He then invited the family to share stories and memories. Andy smiled fleetingly as he remembered Cilla and his wedding, their move to Townsend, and Cilla's coy smile as she let him know she was going to have a baby. "I picked her up and twirled her around that spring afternoon. You know, Abby's birth changed us both, bringing a new kind of love we had never imagined." He choked up and began to sob. Several others in the room started crying.

He took a breath and recomposed himself a bit. "Billy's birth was much more difficult. He was born early, and we both worried he might not be OK, given how tiny he was. But he grew and grew, so rambunctious, so funny.

"Not many people know," Andy continued. "We learned a few weeks ago that Cilla was pregnant with our third child. We planned to let you and the rest of the family know after Christmas."

Cilla's sisters gasped and started to sob. Christine, through her tears asserted, "So there were four people murdered. That brute took four lives."

Emotions spilled over with tears and anger. It took some time for the group to refocus and continue the planning. When they did, Andy declared, "I think I want to speak at the funeral."

"Do you think that is a good idea? Is it even possible?" asked Pastor Lund.

"That is what I want to do. I've gotten clear on that. But, you're right. I think there has to be a back up plan if I can't."

"I can arrange that," Lund assured.

After the meeting, Andy, various parts of the family, and some of the closest friends gathered in a big house in Townsend for lunch. Huddling with loved ones seemed to be the only way to cope with the ongoing barrage of the search, the sounds of helicopters, dogs, sirens, and loud voices intruding and then fading away. What didn't fade was the anguish, the terror, the shock, the disorientation.

All gathered were grieving. Beth and Christine had lost a sister, a niece and nephew. "What if I had been with Cilla and the kids that day? Maybe we would have gone someplace and not have been in the house when LaPlante got in," Christine wondered, in both guilt and horror.

"Will we ever feel safe again in our own home?" friends asked.

"Why couldn't it have been me instead of them?" Andy moaned.

Andy often reverted to staring into space, becoming startled when someone came over to talk with him. Sometimes, in the room, someone's voice grew loud in anger, "If I could get my hands on that Daniel LaPlante!" Sometimes, someone broke into sobs and moans loud enough to quiet the room. But there was laughter, too, as people shared stories of happier times, of sitting around the campfire at the Saco River, of covering the children with sand at the beach on Cape Cod.

Townspeople responded to law enforcement pleas for information with a flood of possible sightings of LaPlante. It is unclear how many of these were real. Certainly, by midday Thursday, LaPlante was cold and hungry. Though law enforcement didn't know it then, he had made a shelter near the edge of a development in Pepperell, Massachusetts, less than a mile through the woods from his West Elm Street home. Accomplished at house break-ins, he succeeded at getting into one of the three homes he attempted to enter, ransacking it, stealing a .32 caliber revolver, some food, and a coat, before returning to his hiding place to spy on the movement around those houses.

That afternoon he spotted sixteen-year-old Pamela Makela leaving in an orange van. He moved closer to that house. When the Volkswagen returned, LaPlante bolted from his hiding place and accosted her before she got into the house. Waving the newly stolen gun in her face, he demanded food and a ride to Fitchburg. Makela recognized LaPlante from the sketches on the news, understood the danger, and negotiated the line between complying with his requests and vigilantly looking for an escape route. She handed him some food from the family kitchen and the two got into the van. She proceeded cautiously, rehearsing in her mind the topography of the upcoming journey toward Fitchburg. She slowed to stop at a light, jumped out of the vehicle, leaving the keys in the ignition, and rolled into a ditch out of the line of sight from the van. LaPlante, frustrated, moved into the driver's seat, and sped away. Pamela ran to the nearest house to call police. LaPlante recognized the implication of the intensive hunt, police cars and state trooper vehicles hiding in every niche and corner. He abandoned the van and returned to moving on foot. The police found the orange van and passed the finding on through their communication network. He couldn't be far.

More than fifty law enforcement officers, from the FBI to the police departments of neighboring towns, engaged in the hunt. They fanned out around the area where the van had been found, going door to door. It was an officer from a neighboring town and another from the Department of Motor Vehicles who lifted the top of the dumpster at an Ayer lumberyard. They found the wiry Daniel hiding in the trash. He surrendered without a fight.

At the home where Andy and his extended family gathered, his friend answered yet another phone call. Turning to Andy, he passed on the message. "This is Assistant District Attorney Tom Reilly. He asked to speak to you. He said it was important."

Somewhat in a daze, Andy took the phone, listened, and stuttered, "Good, good. Thank you for calling."

Hanging up, he shouted, "They caught him," with a cheer that quickly changed into a wail. The room swirled with emotions from rage to relief. As Andy calmed, he repeated the few details given. "Just an hour ago—in a dumpster in Ayer—he just surrendered."

As reactions ricocheted around the room, and the noise level made hearing difficult, Cilla's brother William's booming voice called the group together. "This is a time we should pray." And the room quieted.

"Our Father, You are our God, our Rock and Redeemer, You are the Good Shepherd who leads us through the Valley of Death. We thank You for Your Presence in this time of trouble. We have cried out to You in our fear, in our distress, and You have guided law enforcement to find and capture Daniel LaPlante. Thank You. Thank You that Daniel is now in custody. Thank You for all the people who made this capture possible. But, Lord, our pain and sorrow are great, beyond our ability to manage. Please stay close. Hear our prayers, spoken and unspoken."

After a few moments, others added spoken prayers, tears, and sighs that prayed without words. The Holy Spirit pulsed, drawing the room together, and grounding them in a practice built over a lifetime. William spoke again, "We pray for the LaPlante family and even for our enemy, young Daniel. May we forgive him as You forgive us. We thank You God, and praise You." He took a breath and then, almost automatically, invited everyone to join him in praying as Jesus taught. In the moments that followed the amen, Andy's voice rose in anger, "No, you're wrong! LaPlante is condemned to hell, forever. I will not forgive that man. I will not! I cannot forgive him for what he did to my family." He sobbed, and pounded his fist while the room froze in silent grief.

Toward evening the family and friends gathered dispersed back to their homes. They would reconvene on Saturday morning.

The God who Cries with Us

A ndy decided he would stay in Townsend, accepting the invitation of a friend to move into a room in their house for the time being. Other friends, accompanied by a police escort, went to his house to pick up clothes and personal belongings. Someone was always close by if he wanted to talk or needed anything, but Andy was most likely to sit and stare, almost in a trance, sometimes crying, but often just staring into space. If someone came over to him, especially if they reached to touch him, he would jump, and might even swing his arm. "Easy," came the response. And then Andy would sob or wail.

He thought a lot about how Cilla handled the difficult times of her life, particularly when her father contracted cancer. Her father pastored a church in the Berkshires, and her mother wanted the help of the children in the midst of that crisis, especially Cilla, who had for many years been part of the pastoral team. Cilla loved her parents, and yet reeled under their demands. She left the choir and her Sunday School teaching in Townsend to be with them on the weekends, but missed the time she would ordinarily have spent with Andy and the children. Andy remembered how they prayed together during those months. They would always begin by praising God and offering thanksgiving for something from the day, no matter what. Then they would bring those conflicts to Jesus, naming all the different feelings, their questions, the contradictions of demands, and the unresolvable dilemmas. He remembered Cilla saying: "Sometimes in the midst of pain and anguish God is closer than in good times, but that doesn't mean there will be a quick resolution. Sometimes, you just have to trust God and open to the Presence." He could almost hear her whispering that into his ear now.

Could he do that now? Could he spew out his rage, his grief, his brokenness to Jesus? Cilla, Abby, and Billy were not coming back. Yet, in his sobbing, he had the sense that he was surrounded by love, held by a Presence that he couldn't quite name.

Andy spoke with the area minister, the Rev. Dick Sparrow, by phone. Dick listened as Andy sputtered out some of the details of the murders, and of his thinking about Cilla's spiritual strength, about the joy his family had shared, about the blessings that had been lost. "I am grateful that I have known love, the love we shared. I want to hold on to that and never let it go." When he ended the phone call, Andy put on his coat and walked outside in the darkness until his feet were numbed with cold and his tears turned to ice crystals, until finally, spent, he returned to sleep in snatches through the night.

Moment by moment, hour by hour, Andy prepared for the funeral.

That cold first Saturday in December, the streets lining the Townsend Common filled quickly with cars. Anderson Funeral Home's two hearses stood empty in front of the columned church. A cadre of news trucks was parked on side streets, and police blocked reporters to ensure undisturbed passage for the people arriving at the brick-faced Congregational Church for the funeral for Cilla, Abby, and Billy. People of all ages—including families with young children--streamed into the church. For many, Cilla was their child's preschool teacher, who shared in the nurture of their children, who supported their parenting, who delighted in the growth of each son or daughter. The children had lost a beloved teacher, even though they didn't understand what that meant. Some knew the husband and wife from washing dishes at church dinners, or from Couple's Club discussions. Others knew Andy as an affable, generous lawyer. The wider circles of the church, the town officers, and the legal community were well represented. This devastating loss, overwhelming and seemingly impossible in this place, stunned the community and forced the recognition that violence can happen anywhere.

Every pew was filled, men in suits or state troopers in uniform sitting next to young mothers holding children on their laps. For some, this was the first funeral and perhaps even the first worship service they had attended. For others, this was their church home. Carole Seaver, a church member, arrived ten minutes before the service began, climbed the stairs to the balcony, and found one last seat near the organ. The organist was already playing the prelude. She flashed back to her husband's funeral held here almost three years before. People who arrived after Carole stood in the hallway, spilling out onto the front steps of the church, straining to hear, offering their prayers, expressing their grief, finding what consolation they could from the company of others who, like them, stood shocked, helpless, and sorrowful.

Three shiny white caskets clustered together on the red carpet at the front of the square sanctuary. Three white caskets before the altar, one large and two small, surrounded by multi-colored garlands and fragrant bouquets—carnations, roses, daffodils, birds of paradise—arrangements marked with ribbons reading Wife—Sister—Daughter—Grandson. The Rev. Lund, dressed in a formal black robe, stood as the room became still. After offering opening words, he invited those gathered to stand, to sing, to pray, to remember the promises of God. From the choir loft, Cilla's two sisters and brother sang their love, their grief, and their faith.

Andy had told the area minister, Dick Sparrow, and Pastor Neal Lund that he wanted to speak, that he would try to speak in the service, but no one imagined that he really would, indeed that he really could. Yet, about half way through the funeral, to many people's surprise, Andy rose from his pew, and walked to the pulpit. A hush fell over the congregation. These were Andy's first public words since the tragedy.

"How could God allow such a thing to happen to these beautiful people?"

He uttered aloud the question on everyone's heart.

Then he answered his own question. "I tell you, it wasn't God that allowed this to happen. Never, ever say this was God's will. God loves us, and showers us with all good things. I know that God is crying and mourning with us."

Sparrow reflected later, "It was the word we needed to hear because he asked the question we were asking. And he gave us the answer God wanted us to hear. It would have been very helpful coming from the pastor, but coming from the husband of Cilla, and the father of Billy and Abby, it touched my spirit. It touches me now thinking back all these years."

Andy continued by testifying to the power of love in his family, "a love so strong, so deep, that it can never be taken away." Tears flowed freely, muffled cries arose from different corners, and many clutched the hands of pew mates they hardly knew as Andy continued, struggling to maintain his composure enough to finish saying goodbye to his closest family, these three people who had taught him about love beyond his wildest imagination. "What Cilla and Abby and Billy and I had can never be taken away. Every day we kissed and hugged, and told each other 'I love you.' It could never have been better because it was the best. Our love is stronger than any hate or evil." [3]

Tears now unstoppable, Andy returned to his pew as some people murmured, "We love you, Andy," and "God bless you, Andy." But for most, there were sighs too deep for words, an unbearable grief. Andy cried through the rest of the service, cradled in the arms of his father. With the final blessing, the crowd filed out the front door. On the way out, Carole Seaver spoke to one of Andy's closest friends, offering her help to Andy when and if the time was right. Because she was close to his age and three years along the lonesome road of grief after her husband died, perhaps her experience and listening would be useful.

Andy remained in the sanctuary long after the organ stopped playing, his father's arm around his shoulder. Pastor Lund went to the front steps offering to speak with reporters who were swarming around the building. Pictures of the Rev. Lund and the church flashed across television screens, and his words replayed again and again in newscasts from Boston to Los Angeles. Inside the church, in a time of final parting, Andy lingered at his wife's casket, and then put his hand on each of the children's shiny white beds before he left by the back door, accompanied by his father. The funeral home took the caskets to be cremated, the burial at the cemetery to be held privately at a later time.

The Darkest Days

During the brutal first weeks following the funeral, Andy's large frame collapsed inward. Hour after hour, day after day, he would sit as if in a trance, memories swirling in his mind without logic or connection. Tuesday was Abby's eighth birthday, or it would have been. Andy remembered her gifts, hidden in the closet, and the first sleepover party planned for Saturday, a time when the giggles of little girl friends would have filled the house.

Andy recalled last summer's trip to Disneyland, trying to hold onto the laughter and closeness they felt in those days, circling on the merry-go-round and riding the cars on "It's a Small World." The first night of the vacation, the family had been shaken from sleep by an earthquake, and the hotel alarm system instructed everyone to leave the building. They had huddled outside, surviving the earthquake together, and within an hour or two, everything went back to normal. This time, it would not.

A little more than a week after the murder, Daniel LaPlante was brought before Ayer District Court Judge Joseph T. Travaline, who remanded him to Bridgewater State Hospital for psychiatric evaluation. The police called Andy to request identification of some of the items found in the search: knickknacks, a portable phone, and the Statue of Liberty coin box. The courts released details about new evidence: ammunition, various pieces of clothing, and a fishing knife, fueling more news releases. Some reporters, given a lead on Andy's whereabouts, knocked on doors trying to get an interview with him. The owner of the house where he was staying, answered the door saying, with a straight face, "I have no idea where he is." Later she would add, "I had no idea whether he was in the bathroom or the bedroom." Ten days after the murder, the judge sealed the case, and the pace of reporting slowed. Robert Casey, the LaPlante's family lawyer, sought additional time at Bridgewater, hoping for evidence of insanity, and requesting information from the public that would help his client.

December days, with the lights and songs of the season, could bring Andy back to the practiced anticipation of Christmas, with images of past trees, gift-wrapped presents, family gatherings, and children's joy, but then he would collide with reality. My family is dead, murdered. I am alone, without purpose. Should I even be alive? Day after day, he slouched on the couch or lay on his bed, intermittently bursting into tears, sobbing, sniffling, then—almost as abruptly— calming into a vacant stare. He tried to eat what was served, the food he usually loved, but found he pushed it around with his fork, rarely eating more than a few bites. He walked to his law office, and if he could go in at all, he could stay for only a few minutes. He'd tried to read, but he couldn't concentrate. He would fiddle with small objects he found in his pocket or picked up from a table. He paced. Days were bad, but nights were worse. Sleep, if it came at all, was fitful, filled with flashbacks or nightmares of deep emptiness and monsters.

Day or night, he often spiraled into dark questioning. Why live? The question haunted him, a pain he shared with only his closest companions. He doubted everything he had ever believed: his faith, his relationship with God, his commitment to live a fruitful life. Although his family and friends surrounded him, although he was held in prayer, although he tried to reach out to God in fits and starts, he was beyond help. No one could touch his pain, his isolation, his agonizing suffering.

But for some people, this kind of suffering leads to a deeper relationship with God, a God who suffers with us and in us, whose Presence with us gradually guides the tentative next steps. That would be Andy's journey, although he didn't know it right then. He had drawn on the waters of faith in his years with Cilla, and he slowly began to draw on that well more fully than he had ever done before. Initially, that took the form of setting small goals, small steps toward living: going to the store, reading some of the sympathy cards that piled on the desk in his room, listening to a track of a comedy album. He took small steps, tiny steps toward stability, only to be thrown off balance again and again by yet another trigger he couldn't always identify. Still, each day had moments of peace as well as hours of despondency.

Small blessings appeared. Once or twice in December, Andy talked to Carole Seaver, who had offered her support on the grief journey. She reassured him that he would not cry all of the time forever. Friends offered the use of their cottage on Martha's Vineyard. Andy was part owner of a private plane and could use the Cessna. It was a short flight and the Vineyard cottage became a place of refuge, even for a day or two, if flying could be done by line of sight. Andy was not certified to fly using instruments, so watching the weather was crucial. But flying had always given him a sense of freedom and a big-picture perspective.

He found he could read bits of the Bible, just as he had done in blocks of time since he was a teenager. Sometimes he read favorite texts, sometimes a random verse or two, sometimes passages that he had all but memorized. He found the first verses of the Gospel of John sustained him.

In the beginning was the Word, and the Word was with God, and the Word was God. He was in the beginning with God. All things came into being through him, and without him not one thing came into being. What has

come into being in him was life, and the life was the light
of all people. The light shines in the darkness, and the
darkness did not overcome it.   John 1: 1-5 NRSV

He found the fifth verse offered him the most hope. "The
Light shines in the darkness and the darkness did not overcome
it." He said it to himself again and again.

As days passed, Andy claimed his need to find some way to
move on from living in his friends' bedroom. An acquaintance,
now in Florida for the winter, offered Andy the use of her small
apartment in the center of Townsend. His friends agreed it was
time for him to move; on the other hand, they didn't think he
should be alone. A circle of people worked together to provide almost constant support. His parents, sister, or brother often stayed
with him. His friends did everything they could: going to the
house to pick up needed items, doing his shopping, making sure
someone was around most of the time just to listen if he wanted
to talk. The Couples Club set up a schedule, inviting him to one
of their houses for dinner every night for a year, going to pick
him up if that was needed. He didn't always go, but he knew that
opportunity was always available.

When the police finally finished the investigation at the
Saunders Road house, church members arranged for a cleaning
company to scrub the house, to empty the refrigerator of all per-
ishable foods, to remove the master bedroom mattress, replacing
it with a new one. It was church people who turned down the
heat, checked it when it was cold and plowed the driveway on
those snowy December days. Andy also appreciated the kindness
shown by acquaintances and strangers. Receiving a collection of
handmade cards from a parochial school class of third graders,
and the accompanying note from the nun who was their teacher, moved Andy deeply. He repeated aloud words from that card,
"God's reach is wide."

Andy asked that the church people bring him the devotional material that was located in the Saunders Road bedroom: two Bibles he and Cilla had read together, the folder of study booklets, the notebook in which they wrote their prayers of thanksgiving and hope. One of the Bibles was the one his sister Karen had given him when he was twelve, a version that printed the words Jesus spoke in red ink, the one he had read almost every night in junior and senior high, even before he dated Cilla. The other one was Cilla's personal Bible, given to her by her parents when she was in fourth grade. Andy found it hard to open either of these Bibles to read, and he was more apt to just clutch them to his heart and cry, to touch again the feeling of being together in prayer. He knew he had to learn to draw from her strength and teaching in order to carry this practice on into the future.

It had been less than a month since the murders when Christmas came. Andy spent time with both families, as was the family tradition. The celebrations were subdued, but there were decorated trees and bountiful meals at the gathering of Cilla's family and the extended Gustafson clan. There was more crying than singing, as everyone involved had been deeply wounded by the events in Townsend. Andy did enjoy some of the roast beef and fixings, but he left to take a long walk before dessert was served. When he returned, he ate some Christmas cookies and, for a moment, enjoyed the sweetness.

The Cold of January

The first month anniversary passed as the new year began: January 1988. Andy lived by himself in the small, borrowed apartment, shared dinner with a cycle of friends most nights, and occasionally played poker. Townsend Congregational Church had been central in his life with Cilla and the children. Now, church people provided a constant stream of support for him. Nevertheless, these days Andy found attending worship and activities very difficult. It stirred too many memories, and made losses too clear. Cilla was not singing in the choir, the children did not sit with him at the beginning of the service, the words to the hymns sent too many memories cascading. He might slip into the back pew, but he would leave part way through the service when the tears just wouldn't stop.

But Andy also had a deeply ingrained sense of responsibility. He was the moderator, the non-clergy person in leadership in the church. He chaired the leadership group and the meetings where the whole church gathered to make decisions. The annual meeting of the congregation, which reviewed programs, projects, and spending from the previous year and voted funding for the upcoming season, was held in January. Six weeks after the murder, Andy carried out his role as moderator. He called the meeting to order, performed the beginning routine of naming the purpose of the gathering, determining a quorum, and accepting the minutes from the last meeting. He then turned the leadership over to Pastor Lund, who guided the rest of the agenda.

Andy was less successful at legal work, finding it difficult to concentrate, taking mid-day walks to cry and clear his head, sleeping at odd hours if he could sleep at all. His real estate business partner got impatient as little progress was made to refurbish the hotel in Gardner. The other lawyer in his office, who was his cousin Tom, and their paralegal, Marianne, were much more compassionate with Andy, giving him tasks he could manage and picking up the slack. But since law income is directly related to work that is done, his income plummeted. Andy didn't seem to care, since he now had no family to support.

Cilla and the children never left his thinking. He intentionally rehearsed favorite memories. One recurring memory was of their wedding day, in June of 1975. He could picture the stately stone Congregational church in Great Barrington, so grand on the outside, and always a bit cool and damp inside, even though the stained glass windows streamed colored beams from the bright sun. As the wedding began, Cilla's father, the Rev. Bill Morgan, stood proudly in front of a gathering of friends and family in his Geneva robe. Andy wore the fashion that Cilla wanted, that awful beige bell-bottom suit. He was secretly jealous that his brother Larry got to wear a more traditional darker one. Cilla's sisters had bought their bridesmaid dresses—two different colors of the same style—at the discount department store, Zayres. How proud they were to promenade down the aisle as the pipe organ labored over the Bridal Chorus. But the big reveal was next.

He remembered holding his breath as the congregation stood and turned in anticipation when the back door of the sanctuary flung open. Cilla, in her stunning white lace dress, glowed in the sun with beams of light flashing off her jewelry. Andy's face lit up in the remembering, just as he did that day as Cilla floated toward him. He didn't remember much of the formal ceremony except that they had read First Corinthians 13, with the phrase, "love never dies." That memory brought tears. Will love never die? Even when the people do? My love won't die! I won't forget! Then, out loud, talking to his family, "I will love you always."

Family continued to be primary supporters. Andy's parents came to

Andy as a boy with his siblings, circa 1960.

visit, bringing food and reassurance. His sister Karen drove from Amherst, talked over coffee, played cards, and hiked local trails. He and his brother cross-country skied, mostly around town, but they took a day trip to Northfield Mountain one weekend. The two of them laughed about the weekend that the two couples left the children with the grandparents, and drove to Vermont in the midst of a blizzard. Cilla covered her eyes much of the time, she got so scared about the driving. But when they arrived, they relished their time at the Nutmeg Country Inn, with its fireplaces, hearty breakfasts, great cross-country skiing, and evening alone time. Now Andy's time with extended family provided moments of normalcy.

One evening in January, after the scheduled dinner at a friend's house, Andy invited Carole Seaver over to his apartment for dessert. He thought he might be ready to accept her offer of support, as someone near his age who had experienced the death of a spouse. This began a regular time of talking together. Actually, in the early months of their meetings, Andy did most of the talking, focusing on how to manage the swells of emotions and the challenges of continuing to live. But there were also memories and stories of his life with Cilla and the children.

"In high school, I decided I wanted to be a millionaire and that law would be my path to earning that kind of money. Both Cilla and I grew up in families with limited financial resources and we imagined a life where money would flow freely, but we knew we would have to work hard to get there.

"I enrolled in law school following our wedding, and we rented a third-story walk-up tenement in Worcester, at the bottom of a hill, not far from where my brother Larry and his wife Shelley lived. The small flat with a tiny porch overlooked other tenements and had a clothesline for hanging laundry washed in the bathroom sink. Weekends we often drove home to my parents in West Brookfield, or all the way to the Berkshires to visit hers. We'd get laundry done, eat great dinners, share news, and go to church. During the week, we had a meager budget, but Cilla figured out how to create meals out of Spam fixed a hundred different ways. She had a non-Spam meal for guests, too—egg foo yung with chicken livers. Back then, that was our idea of elegant.

"Cilla sold shoes at Thom McAns at a strip mall close enough to walk to, but she preferred to drive when the car was available. We had this old car given to us by our parents so that I could drive to Boston for law classes. I decided to sell pots and pans door to door to get more money, and I kept the inventory in the car, thinking it would be empty soon. That wasn't a very successful venture, in the end.

"We relied on Larry and Shelley a lot. They came over frequently for cards or company or help. It seemed like once a week we'd call them to rescue us, because the car wouldn't start. As clunky as it was, it wasn't always the car's fault. We'd do something wrong, like lock the keys in the car or leave the headlights on. I think their patience wore thin sometimes, but they would always show up with an extra can of gas, another set of keys, or jumper cables."

But often Andy would tell stories and not be able to finish them, because he would start sobbing. Exercising incredible patience, Carole would sit beside him, sometimes touching his shoulder or holding his hand, but mostly, she would just witness the tears and be present to the pain, letting him know he was not alone and that he was held in the hands of God.

When the tears were finished and he recomposed himself, Carole would reassure him that telling the stories and expressing the feelings were important parts of mourning. And so was having some moments of normalcy, even if it felt disloyal to those who died. Andy usually felt better after he and Carole talked.

The Long Road Home

Many of Andy's memories centered around the house on Saunders Road. Sometime in January, he decided to go home again in order to reconnect with this source of strength and love, announcing his intention to family and friends. He created a plan of successive approximation, of desensitization, in which he would drive Route 119 headed toward the house, intentionally focusing his mind on positive memories, doing what he could to combat the strong negative ones from the tragedy. He'd remember how Cilla and he searched for a place to live after law school. When they first caught sight of the central common in Townsend, they both thought of the green triangle in their hometown of West Brookfield. This was it, they thought. At first, they couldn't find an affordable apartment, so they took one in the neighboring town of Ashby, and went looking for a piece of land on which they could build, one in their price range. That is where Andy had first met his current business partner, the speculative real estate broker.

He could hold the positive memories only so long, before the flashbacks intruded, the tears began to flow, and the pain became intolerable. He would stop and turn around, but he would repeat the journey in the next day or two, going farther each time.

Finally, he turned onto his dead-end street, but before he could take the winding road far enough to see his house, the flashbacks to that December evening overtook him. Nevertheless, his determination to return to the house grew stronger. That night, he talked about this experience with Carole, posing the questions circulating in his head.

"I want to turn that corner and drive by the house. I just want take a quick peek, but I don't know if I am ready. The terrible images just explode in my mind."

"Just the terrible memories?" Carole asked. "Aren't there other memories, too?"

Andy sat in silence and then his body shifted, a smile crossed his face, and his tone changed. "You're right. I remember this funny scene on our driveway. When we bought that land, there was no road to the part of the property where we built the house. We had to create a road several hundred yards long. So we built a narrow dirt drive just wide enough for one car. One day, a fully loaded oil truck came to make a delivery and slid off the road. Its front wheels dangled in the air over the gully. It took two tow trucks to pull it out. What a mess! Didn't save any money by that decision. I think Cilla tossed out an 'I told you so.'"

Carole smiled. "We all do stupid things, don't we? But that house, the two of you invested so much in it, building a nest of love for your family. Remember, that is why you want to reclaim it. This is important and you can do it."

The next day, he did drive by the house. Yes, he cried and there were some bad memories, but the good memories won out that day. He accomplished his first goal of glimpsing his home. It would be many more weeks with many steps before he would open the front door.

Near the end of January, the Middlesex grand jury handed down twenty-eight indictments against Daniel LaPlante, including the November burglary of the Gustafsons' house and the murders of Cilla, Abby, and Billy. LaPlante, back from almost a month of psychiatric observation, pleaded not guilty to all charges.

This announcement threw Andy back into anger, terror, and

depression. Enraged, he roared, "How can he think he is not guilty? How could he be so cruel, so callous? Why did it have to be these beautiful people? Why did they let him out on bail earlier, anyway?" But that was better than when he turned those feelings inward. "Why couldn't I have saved them? Why should I keep living? What is the purpose? Everything I love is destroyed—I think I'll take my car, and drive into a tree." He spoke these things out loud to those closest in his life, to his sister and brother, to his most trusted friends, to Carole in the long evening conversations.

His family and friends aimed to be available to him any time of day or night, but no one could really touch his pain. Carole drew on her own experience, offering practical, insightful reassurance. She would remind him to just get through this day. "Grief clouds our thinking. It will get better, it just takes time, a lot of time," she asserted. "Remember how Cilla taught you about hope. Draw on that hope now. Isn't that what she'd say to you?"

One January night following a time with Carole, Andy pulled out a card from among the Bible study materials that he and Cilla had used at difficult times, such as when her father was dying or she felt conflicted in her relationship with her mother, or when she and Andy disagreed or struggled about money. It wasn't that their life had always been perfect. He and Cilla had gotten through difficult seasons. Andy found one of the verses Cilla referred to in times like that, Romans 12:12. "*Rejoice in hope, be patient in tribulation, be constant in prayer.*" He said that one over and over to himself in the days that followed, almost the way Cilla whispered a verse in their bedtime rituals.

He came to rely on conversations with Carole to keep him going, day to day. The focus was typically daily thoughts and feelings, particularly those things that triggered grief, or the desire to share stories of his former life. But, intermittently, Andy wanted to know more about Carole. Carole and her husband, Greg belonged to the Townsend church. He knew that Greg had had brain cancer, and had died three years before. He and Cilla had prayed for them, brought meals as part of the church's support, attended the funeral, and visited Carole the Christmas following his death. But really, he didn't know much about her, didn't know her story. He could see that Carole loved Greg deeply and missed him profoundly. She would light up when she remembered the good times, just as Andy did, but he recognized that there was so much more to know.

Gradually, in fits and starts, Andy asked Carole more specific questions about her life. Over time, they found places they were alike, and many places where their experiences differed widely. Whereas Andy grew up in one house and one town, Carole grew up in a military family that moved frequently. She married Greg, an army hospital administrator with an expertise in establishing MASH units, a task very important during the Vietnam War but less important in peacetime. Carole had seen much more of the world than Andy. She had worked as a civilian at various army bases, following Greg as he moved from post to post.

Carole and Greg Seaver, circa 1969

"How did you come to Townsend?" Andy asked one evening after sharing how he and Cilla had dreamed and looked before selecting Townsend as their home.

"As Greg approached the end of his tenth year in the army, we weighed leaving or aiming for the twenty-year mark," Carole recalled. "He quietly put out his resumé, and landed a civilian job as an administrator of the Fernald School in Waltham. We wanted to settle down, find and fix up an old house, and start a family. We found the colonial on the green in Townsend that fit our dream."

By February, Andy and Carole were meeting regularly. The conversations were going deeper. Andy began describing his difficulty sleeping, and, little by little, shared some of his dreams. There were flashbacks to the murders, and nightmares with monster-like creatures inflicting torture and terror. But there were also pleasant dreams. One evening, Andy shared that Cilla, Abby, and Billy had come to him in his dream state. Each of them had stood by his bed; he had felt their touch, heard them speak, reassured by words such as these: "I love you." "We're all right, Dad, really. We have no pain and no fear." And, "We are close by you, guiding you."

He often smiled as he told these stories, and then, without notice, could turn and start sobbing. "I miss them so much. How can I continue to live without them?" Carole would sit there and witness his speaking and his tears, mostly without words. When he would begin to emerge from the emotions, she would reassure him that this was all part of the grief journey. She never questioned Andy's need to move randomly among pain, guilt, sorrow, and anger, and then turn to recall memories that sprang to mind. Friends and family had done this for her. Now she was passing along the gift.

Cars, Planes, and Jig Saws

In early February, Andy wanted to go to a concert in Boston, a little less than an hour's drive away. He invited Carole to go with him. That night, Carole discovered something new about Andy, something that had been whispered about at church, something she had never really taken seriously. "Andy drives recklessly. Be careful!"

As they traveled the narrow, winding Route 119, Andy exceeded the speed limit until he would come up behind a slower car. Then, he'd hug its bumper, ride his brakes, and peek out into the passing lane, sometimes barely avoiding oncoming traffic. With the slightest possible amount of room, he would suddenly accelerate to pass, periodically causing an oncoming car to swerve or slam on its brakes. Carole's knuckles were white as she clutched the edge of her seat. They made it to Boston and enjoyed the concert, but it took most of the evening for her to relax. She hoped Andy would be more focused and at ease now, but the drive home was worse, with even more extreme cycles of speeding and braking. Exasperated, Carole asserted herself. "You may have a death wish, but I do not. Let me out of the car here, if you must continue to drive this way." Andy was taken aback. He looked at her briefly, then changed his behavior and drove home at a steadier pace.

Week after week, Carole listened to Andy explore his inner world: the grief and loss, the struggle to choose to live, the search for meaning, the questions about the future. Work had been turned on its head. Work he had previously enjoyed now overwhelmed him. At times, he found real estate disgusting. In his emotional fog, it was hard to sort out the reasons. Was it the work itself, or was it the relationship with his business partner that was so distasteful? Andy didn't mind working with contractors to refurbish the hotel in Gardner, and the customary legal tasks were OK when he could concentrate. As he sorted through his thoughts and feelings, he realized that he struggled with his partner's ethics. And his own previous goal of making a lot of money now jarred his sensibilities.

But one of the reasons Andy sought money was to support a very expensive hobby, flying. He had dreamed of flying since he was a boy, and co-owning the plane with his business partner was a dream come true, or so he had thought.

Andy and Billy with plane

It now was tied to some guilt. He thought of the night he came home to tell his plan to Cilla. "I remember how my business partner spoke gloriously of flying his small plane, a Cessna, housed at the Fitchburg airport. I know I asked a lot of questions, about cost, about ease of flying, about upkeep. One day, he tossed out the idea that we could share ownership of the plane. It would be one of the benefits of the partnership, he said. The costs could be deducted from the payments due. This was like a dream come true. I could own my own plane. Well, co-own. So, I said yes. Yes, without even discussing it with Cilla. I feel guilty now, because money was always tight and we had usually made decisions like this together.

"When I told her that night, I could see in her face that she was stunned and disappointed in me, but her words focused on my dreams—my dreams, not our dreams. She celebrated this, for me. Did I do as well for her? I don't know."

Carole reminded him, "You can celebrate her love for you. She loved you. Don't ever forget that."

"As I think about it, airplanes have been a kind of obsession in my life, a seduction, even. As a teen, I used paper-route money to take a flight in a Piper Cub and I got hooked. I would become a pilot. And I did, even though it was expensive, and I had to pay for it myself. I had enough paper route money saved to do a couple of lessons. I stopped going to Boy Scouts, despite my father's objections. I took a job as janitor of the machine shop across from the church, a job that would pay for lessons, a job that ultimately helped fund college. It was all worth it to learn to control the aircraft, to feel the freedom of flying. It took me more than a year, but I earned my student pilot license while I was in high school, complete with the ritual of the shirt being torn off my back and mounted on the wall. Later, I passed my private pilot license. I felt like I could do anything."

He paused and sighed. "We have a whole lot less control of our lives than we think we have when we are teenagers."

During these days, Andy continued his step-by-step progress toward reclaiming his house. Small steps: stopping at the end of the driveway, inching up the drive day after day, sitting in the parked car outside of the house, getting out of the car to just stand there, looking at the flower bed, walking to the back yard, and glimpsing the swing set. So many memories flooded him in these visits:

the laughter in the mornings and at bedtimes, the sacred ritual of evening prayer time with Cilla, the challenge of building the house itself, and all the help he got from family in the process. In retrospect, Andy recognized the comedy of some of their home-building efforts.

"We hired a building contractor to lead the basic work, but decided to do some pieces of finish work ourselves, to save money. My mother, Shirley, a master of wallpaper, brought primer, measuring tools, wallpaper trays, and utility knives. I remember schlepping them from the car to the house and back again. She and Cilla picked out wallpaper and borders. How they loved to flip through those big books they brought home from the hardware store. Mom came to the house for months to finish the task. I need to thank her again for all that work. She is such a supporter.

"Cilla wanted to stencil the walls, adding the same design to the curtains for our dream house, which she ultimately finished in one room. I want to see those again, even the ones with some of the paint blobs outside the intended design. It just added to her creativity. Sweet.

"I decided to do the wood trim with my brother Larry. 'How hard could it be?' I thought." He laughed out loud, still a rare occurrence.

"Well, it turns out that cutting molding with the precise angle needed to fit snugly at the corner is not as easy as it looks, especially for someone like me who wasn't all that good at using an electric jigsaw." He winced, remembering. "I cut into the electrical cord, stopping the machine cold, and making a big spark."

Carole's jaw dropped. "You did what?" She broke out laughing.

"Well, you reacted better than Cilla, who was totally exasperated with me. She got a church friend to teach me how to use a miter box, adding a side serving of humility."

Finally came the day when he walked up the steps and unlocked the door, going no further. That night, when Carole and he talked, they celebrated and spoke of the love in the house. A couple of nights later, when Andy unlocked the door and actually stood in the kitchen, he decided to invite Carole to fix the first dinner in the house together. A couple of days later, they did just that.

Andy and his poker group reclaimed the house by moving their game back to Saunders Road. The first time, Andy went with the group, opened the door, and they all entered together. The following week or two, he went first, turned on the heat, and greeted his buddies as they arrived. Soon thereafter, he moved back into the house.

"I had to emotionally reclaim it," Andy said in a later interview. "I had to go back in there and be all right. The house became a source of strength for me, with the memories of my family. The love that occurred there was much stronger than the death there."

Carole's Story

By now, Andy was going to church every Sunday and attending the church leadership meetings. The meetings felt normal, although worship still brought him to places of grief and mourning. He talked with Carole about his growing involvement in church life.

One night he was curious about Carole's journey with the church. "How did you get involved with Townsend Congregational?"

Carole smiled in remembering. "It started the day that the moving truck unloaded our furniture. Greg and I guided the movers, pointing to where items needed to be placed, unpacking boxes into kitchen shelves, carrying clothes to hang in closets. This pleasant man with a big smile knocked on our door and said, 'I've brought you coffee. I figured you would need some about now.' He had everything we needed: paper cups, a bag with sugars and creamers, lots of coffee, and a second bag with donuts.

"We were surprised and grateful for the hospitality. We found three chairs and used the kitchen counter as a shelf because the table hadn't arrived yet.

"He said he'd always wanted to see the inside of the house, and told us the house used to be the parsonage for the church down the street. Greg and I delighted in pointing out all the quirky things we had already fallen in love with in the house.

"After the house tour, the man made one more generous offer. He invited us to dinner, adding, 'It has to be simple, probably burgers, because my wife has had surgery recently. But I think she would enjoy getting to know our neighbors better, too.'

"Gratefully, we accepted, and asked where he lived.

"'Down there, next to the church,' he gestured. 'My name is John Mingus. I'm the pastor of the church. Oh, by the way, we'd love to have you come to worship on Sunday, too, if you'd like.'

"We had dinner together and did go to the church the following Sunday. We never went anywhere else in Townsend."

"We loved John Mingus, too," mused Andy. "Cilla felt connected to him, and was sad when he left Townsend. Mingus recognized her gifts––of music, of writing prayers, of being with children. But more than that, Cilla confided her worries and struggles to him. John Mingus was such a good listener, and gave her fresh perspectives. When her father had the stroke and her mother increased her demands, he offered insights into the dynamics of pastors' families that loosened Cilla's feelings of guilt. They prayed together, reminding her to be thankful and to listen deeply to God in the midst of trouble. She would come home and share how much more peaceful she felt. He would strengthen Cilla's spiritual practice, and she would bring it home, helping us both grow in following Jesus.

"And can you tell me more about Greg's cancer?" Andy asked

"Yes," Carole nodded and thought for a moment. "I'll begin on the day of the home inspection at the Townsend house. While coming downstairs following the inspector, Greg hit his head on the overhang, hit his head hard. He put ice on it, but did not stop working. That night, he slept at his brother's house, north of Boston. The next morning, he found himself on the floor, and, in conversation with his brother, realized that he had had a seizure in the night. That had never happened before. He thought banging his head was the cause. But when a few days later he had a second seizure, he went for an evaluation. This led to a neurological work-up at Mass General. When it was time to review the results, the doctor left me in the waiting room, and met with Greg alone. He had a brain tumor that would be dangerous to remove surgically. The doctor advised treating the seizures with Dilantin, monitoring the growth of the tumor, and waiting for more advances in neurosurgery. But it was already clear, the dream we imagined, with children and a happy, long life, was evaporating."

"So you know what that's like," Andy interrupted. Carole went on.

"The treatment worked for a while, maybe a year. I got a job at a local human resource office, while Greg worked as a hospital administrator. The doctors experimented with different drug cocktails to control the headaches and manage the increasing balance issues. After fifteen months, his health and the personality changes connected with brain tumors ended his career. By then, we had switched our treatment teams to Lahey Clinic, choosing one that would include me as a partner in treatment and decision-making. Once he stopped work, there were almost daily trips for radiation treatment and chemotherapy. It was exhausting.

"Greg lost weight and went bald. He had radiation burns on the side of his face, so he wore his Greek fisherman cap slightly tilted on his head when he went out. His personality changed from the happy-go-lucky, easygoing person I married. That was the toughest challenge. The team discussed the effects of the current treatment versus surgery, weighing the pros and cons of a variety of possible actions. In September of 1982, they proceeded with brain surgery. The neurosurgeon and oncologists at Lahey gave him a six-month prognosis and recommended hospice, allowing me to keep working. That fall and winter after the surgery, Greg was bedridden, his balance so off that he was unsafe out of bed for more than a few steps. But, remarkably, he got better rather than worse. His balanced improved enough that he could sometimes venture out of the house. The church welcomed and celebrated his help as he folded bulletins and newsletters, answered the phone while the secretary picked up the mail, or ironed squares when the quilting group met. He had a purpose. He could help when he was able.

"Greg surpassed the initial six-month prognosis and was doing OK, despite significant balance issues. That's when Greg's parents, accomplished sailors, proposed a trip to the Caribbean. The four of us flew to Tortola, rented a 27 ft yacht and enjoyed the most beautiful blue-green water, strong sun, a delightful breeze and delicious food. Greg didn't want to be an invalid and tried to participate in the sailing, but his balance, unreliable on land, grew worse with rocking seas. But, he could sleep off the discomfort. We relaxed, rested, and reconnected with each other. It was great.

"It was such good timing because Greg deteriorated after the trip. He fell and broke his front teeth. At Halloween, he couldn't cut the jack-o-lantern, so I gently took the knife away. The Thanksgiving trip to my brother's home in Minnesota overwhelmed him. His head hurt constantly. He died a few weeks later, December 11, 1984, after fifteen years of marriage." She took a long breath. Andy squeezed her hand.

Carole's mood shifted. "Did I tell you how supportive the church was during his illness? They offered amazing and consistent support. John Mingus came often. He and Greg had long discussions on every topic imaginable. The interim pastor came almost weekly. Church folk provided a circle of care. The Scouts mowed the lawn and raked the leaves, Roy plowed the driveway without charging us for the service, a cadre of people brought meals several times a week, and Judy Mingus did our laundry in the winter when the washing machine didn't work. People listened. Charlie and Nancy became like second parents to us, and Dave, who had lost his son to brain cancer, answered our questions and gave advice. Cards came in the mail, friends phoned to asked what we needed and people prayed for us and with us."

Andy paused and looked away for a moment. "Yes, a lot of people are caring for me these days, too."

Seeing in Color

By the fourth month after the murders, Andy recognized a routine in his life. He lived on Saunders Road, ate dinner with a round robin of friends, spent time with family and Carole, and reconnected with the church. When the weather forecast had a few decent days, Andy would take the plane and fly to Martha's Vineyard to be by himself, staying at his friend's cottage and walking the beaches. At home, he got some work done at the office, writing some wills, arranging for contractors, doing a few routine real-estate closings. He still cried frequently, got distracted easily, and rarely laughed, but he knew he wasn't alone.

He lived one day at a time. He'd get up, go to the office for the morning, then leave to walk for an hour or more. Sometimes he'd end up at home, at other times back in the office. It was on one of those walks in March, on one of those spring-like days that slip in between the March lion and lamb, one of those days with crystal blue skies, a warm breeze by winter's standards, and hints of a coming spring––it was on such a day that Andy saw color again.

The gray grief that had shrouded him since the murder, through which he perceived everything—that grayness dropped from his vision like scales from his eyes, just for a few minutes. He saw clearly. He saw the colors of nature around him: the rich blueness of the sky, the white patches of snow, the green of the first shoots of flowers to come. He felt the sun's warmth, noticed the gentle breeze, saw the maple buckets collecting the rising sap. How many days of sunshine had he missed in his gloomy state? How had he not seen the glories of nature, the arrival of the first robin, the swelling of the pussy willows?

Then he recognized an emotion that was different from ones that had been his constant companions of late. He felt guilty, guilty that he had lost touch with the world outside him, lost touch with God's creation that kept the sun rising every day, lost the awe of discovering the crocuses poking out through the snow. That feeling passed and the grayness returned, yet this experience marked a turning point in the journey of grief.

Andy prayed more consciously, more directly now, especially on his trips to the Vineyard. He continued to wrestle with his faith, often praying his hidden doubts and pain aloud in the solitude of his beach walks. "How could You, a loving God, allow such evil, such viciousness to exist in the world? Are You all powerful, or even powerful at all?" Sometimes he yelled, cried, kicked stones, or hit his hand with his fist, but mostly he would just walk as he wrestled with these seemingly irresolvable questions. He would shift from prayer to pondering, arguing with himself. "How can I think God is good when God has let bad things happen to my family?" Then he'd contradict himself, reconnecting with the Holy Presence, the steadfastness, the love that was with him and around him, through nature, people, and prayer.

Andy tried to remember what he had learned in church, through preaching and study, about who God was and what God does, through Jesus, through the Holy Spirit, through the mystery of Creation. What he knew for sure was that love was central, but even though Jesus lived that love, had awesome power, and included people at the margins, he was still subjected to a violent death. But that was not the end of the story. Love continued. Somehow the love with Cilla and the children continued, too. He would puzzle these deep questions until he would all but exhaust himself.

Then, it would be as if Cilla would whisper in his ear, "Rest in God." He would walk in silence or repeat some scripture.

> Where can I go from your spirit? Or where can I flee from your presence? If I ascend to heaven, you are there; if I make my bed in Sheol, you are there.
> If I take the wings of the morning and settle at the farthest limits of the sea, even there your hand shall lead me, and your right hand shall hold me fast.
> If I say, "Surely the darkness shall cover me, and the light around me become night," even the darkness is not dark to you; the night is as bright as the day, for darkness is as light to you.
>
> Psalm 139 verses 7-12, NRSV

He connected again with the power of God's Light in the midst of a broken world, with the message that sustained him immediately after the murders. In December, he knew God cried with him, and he did indeed claim that belief publicly when he spoke at the funeral. Now he recognized that God had never left him, even in his darkest moments. The Holy Love was there with his friends and family, with the beauty of creation, with scripture and prayer, with the inner knowing he felt with and around him. For a moment he felt the joy of communion with God.

For several months, Carole listened patiently to Andy and supported his grief journey, but she knew that he needed additional companionship she could not provide, some people whose experience was closer to what he had to manage. District Attorney Tom Reilly had invited Andy to a group for family members of homicide victims, sponsored by the Victim Support Services of the D.A.'s office. Carole encouraged Andy to accept Reilly's offer, sharing how a grief support group for cancer spouses had helped her feel less isolated. Reluctantly, Andy agreed to attend one session, a session where Reilly would speak as a resource person.

When Reilly arrived in Townsend to pick him up, Andy was skittish. "I'm not sure I really want to do this."

Reilly, who had accompanied other loved ones to these meetings, walked a fine line. "Try it out. Just listen. There is no need to speak. I'll do a small talk on resources tonight, and then leave the room, waiting until you are ready to go home. It's your timing, and you will decide whether you return."

Arriving at the building, Andy followed a few steps back from Reilly and, on entry, slunk to the back of the room. The leader and Reilly pulled chairs into a circle, aided by some of the entering group members. The leader called the group together and reviewed the usual schedule for the gathering.

"This is a support group for family members of homicide victims. Leadership is provided by a team of trained counselors who specialize in grief recovery, who are paid by the district attorney's office. One or two of us will be present every week, opening and closing the meeting, providing the structure, but you are the experts in this group. Some people attend for many years, others, only a few times. This group is confidential, meaning what is said here, stays here.

"We begin with voluntary introductions. Then we do a short, focused topic, like hearing about the Victim Compensation resources. Then there will be time for two or three people have something to share—dealing with feelings, preparing for court, sharing a memory, whatever. We finish by sharing and practicing ways people cope.

"So, let's begin. Who would like to introduce themselves?"

Many in the circle did. They spoke of sons and daughters, of husbands and girlfriends, of parents and siblings. People gave names and relationships like an honor court. Andy cried softly, hugging the wall.

Next, D.A. Reilly spoke of victim advocates and financial assistance, of counseling resources and funds for childcare during court testimony. He offered his deep condolences on each person's loss, often using people's names, and reassuring them that although he knew he couldn't really understand their pain, he did care about not leaving them alone to be hurt even further. A few people asked questions, and then he slipped out of the room.

Using a non-verbal signal, the leader cued the group to adjust their chairs to include Andy more completely. Then one member told how she discovered the murder victims in her apartment, step by step, detail by detail, question by question, with tears, rage, and long blocks of sobbing. The group focused their attention and witnessed this pouring out with great compassion. When that person finished, another member came to sit with her until she was ready to emerge from her own feelings.

A second person spoke of preparing for court with all the emotions and questions that stirred. This time, some members offered suggestions and asked more questions.

The leader noted that the ending time was approaching and asked what positive coping or calming device people had tried this week. "I love the spring," one person offered. "I walked in the sun and thought of all the spring games I played with my daughter. I remembered the laughter. So I bought a balloon to take home in honor of her."

"Thank you," chimed in a couple of people. "I like the idea of finding a memento."

The leader said, "I will be here again next week, and there will be another member of the leadership team with us, as well. Know you can come to this gathering on your own schedule. I hope you come again."

Andy whispered to one of the speakers, "I am so sorry for your loss."

The person replied, "I hope you come again. I find this very helpful."

Andy found Reilly, and together they drove back to Townsend. Andy was quiet for a long time and then he volunteered, "Thank you for pushing me. I think I will go back."

Spring Brings New Life

Even though Andy had made progress in reclaiming the house, in returning to church, in sharing his pain with Carole, and in connecting with the grief support group, he still regularly struggled with work and with sleep. He walked to cope and to calm himself, often wandering over to the cemetery, heading toward the stones furthest from the road.

The family's gravestone had been engraved with two Bible verses: "The Light shines in the darkness and the darkness has not overcome it," and, "Love never dies." There he would talk with Cilla and the children the way he had at the dinner table and at bedtime. He basked in the familial closeness, reconnecting with his capacity to love, to care, to live with purpose

Gustafson stone,
taken by Betsy Waters 2014

and meaning. As he walked out of the cemetery, he began to see the names and dates of others who had died, noticing the ages of those buried. It was like an angel on his shoulder pointing, "Look. Look." There were children buried, indeed many other children who had died, many other fathers and mothers who had lost sons and daughters. He was not alone.

His friend's cottage on the Vineyard was another place of prayer and reflection. He spent long hours walking the beach, staring at the ocean, rocking on the porch, listening to the sounds of nature. Here on the island, he felt the presence of Cilla and the children, listened to the deep parts inside himself, and began to imagine choosing a new life. He discovered that he wanted a place on the Vineyard of his own, for the summer as well as winter. He shared this dream with Carole.

Andy attended the support group by himself, joined the circle, but did not introduce himself for a couple of weeks. Instead he listened. As he heard the stories of parents who lost children to gunshots, drownings, and abuse, and of spouses whose partners had died in stabbings, gun battles, and beatings, his heart opened.

Slowly, meeting by meeting, Andy began to tell his story and to share his memories. First, he spoke during the time of introduction. Soon thereafter, he retold coming home on the first of December to find his wife and children dead. He wrestled with the shame he felt at not being home when they needed him, at not being there to protect his family.

One night he talked about his daughter. "Abigail, my beloved Abby. She was born in December of 1979, the most wonderful gift of the season. She was a sweet, smart child, so much like her mother. I loved to read and giggle with her. She had this strange combination of being shy and attracting friends. She had a lovely voice. About a month before the murders, she sang a solo at church. My parents came to hear her sing during worship, and to celebrate Billy's birthday. She was nervous that day. I overheard her say to Cilla, 'Mommy, I'm scared about standing up front.'

"Cilla quietly counseled her. 'I know you will do fine. I remember being scared when I stood up in front of my church, but your grandfather told me that Jesus would be with me, holding my hand.' Abby sang absolutely beautifully, that morning. We and her grandparents were so proud of her."

"That was a full day. My parents brought a birthday present for Billy's fifth birthday. He was so excited. He had to wait until after dinner to open it: a toy helicopter. Billy and Grandpa Len played rescue together on the living room rug. My father always had this uncanny ability to just be present, supportive, and encouraging. And he was there for my children. They loved him so much."

"One of the ways I am coping is writing. I even tried my hand at poetry. Here is one I wrote about Abby."

> Abigail, Abigail
> My source of joy
> You were to my world
> Like the morning sun.
>
> You brightened my days
> You lightened my loads.
> You made me so happy
> You made me so proud.
>
> I know you're still living
> In a form I don't know.
> I know you're still living
> But how I miss you so.
>
> I just want to have just one more T-A-L-K,
> To tickle you faster
> To hold you so close.
>
> Be always my angel
> And watch over me tonight
> As I whisper I love you,
> Goodnight
>   Sleep tight
>   Don't let the bed bugs bite.[4]

(Andy Gustafson, published in the *Boston Globe*, Oct. 9, 1988)

Andy's appreciation of the grief group grew. This was a place where his strong emotions felt reasonable. He could tell the stories again and again and stop and cry, knowing others had some idea of what he was experiencing. In addition, he found that he could offer compassion and listening to other survivors of violence.

Andy stayed connected to Cilla's family, especially her sisters. They were in mourning, with all the multitude of contradictory feelings that involved. Knowing that Christine ruminated, "What if I had been there that day..." Andy shared insights from the grief support group with her. "It is amazing how many people in the group beat themselves up with that question. Christine, the murders were not your fault. You have to believe that in your innermost heart." They would hold each other, both crying until the tears stopped. After a few minutes, they could be telling each other funny or touching memories.

One night at the support group, the leader opened the topic of how the loss of a family member to violence made other people uncomfortable. "This kind of loss each of you has experienced is unnatural and scary. You know that. And people around you—friends, neighbors, loved ones—they often are overwhelmed, terrified, powerless in the face of these feelings. Some cope using denial, which is both self-protective and a block to authentic sharing. It can seem that you make other people uncomfortable. Has anyone experienced this?"

That unleashed a torrent of stories, with head-shaking and seething emotions. One person had been advised, "Get over this. It's been two years already." Another had been asked not to come to a family gathering "until you're ready," because the person cried too often. This led Andy to think about how his friends and community were dealing with their feelings, and their relationship with him. They're right, he thought to himself. The whole town is in shock, not knowing how to deal with this. At one point, Andy added a comment, "I appreciate this group. Here, it is OK to share where I am at the moment, knowing it probably will change in a minute or two. I have learned other people have similar experiences, not just of the murders, but also of the strange world we enter on the other side, with its difficulty concentrating, the fear that another loved one could die unexpectedly, and then, by contrast, this deep appreciation for the joy of the moment."

From the author: When I pastored Andy's church twenty-five years after these days, I found many people avoided conversations about the murders or what happened in the year or two that followed. But what was more surprising was discovering, upon reviewing the newsletters in the six months following the murders, that there were no references to Cilla and the children, no published prayers for Andy, no programming or special worship experiences for the community dealing with grief, no spiritual reflections to guide parents in addressing children's fears. The one prayer that referred to Andy wished him safe travels to England. I have lots of unanswered questions about these observations. Did Andy request that? Was the pastor uncomfortable? Was the newsletter too public to report grief support efforts in the community? Certainly, the support this congregation offered Andy was amazing. Was the congregation offered the grief support they needed? And what would it have looked like if they had been?

Andy returned to the leadership board meetings of the county level of his denomination. In his role on the board of directors of the Central Association, Andy provided legal advice as well as other kinds of leadership. This was a group that stopped to pray together and would talk about how God was in the midst of the work they were doing. Andy found the presence of the area minister, the Rev. Dick Sparrow, particularly helpful. The two of them met for coffee soon after Andy came back to board meetings.

Mostly Dick provided a safe space for Andy to talk. But in a lull, Dick shared a memory. "I was so moved by the funeral service. You asked the question that was on my heart, really on everyone's heart. 'How could God allow such a thing to happen to these beautiful people?'"

They sat in silence for a few moments until Andy started talking about those first days after the murders. He finished by thanking Dick. "I appreciate your listening to me. These memories are so precious."

Dick reflected, "At the last meal with his disciples, Jesus broke the bread and said, 'Do this in remembrance of me.' I think remembering was important to Jesus, and that he knew it would be important to his followers. I wonder what memories the disciples told around the campfire, at the dinner table, or as they walked together. It is right and sacred to share our stories."

Friends began to push Andy and Carole to be a couple. That was the last thing that Carole could imagine. The two of them were markedly different. She kept telling people that. Couldn't they see it? Carole had traveled the world, had a confidence in meeting lots of people, and was reticent to be vulnerable again, especially with someone like Andy, who had a country boy's way, more socially awkward than one would expect of a person who was so well educated, more like a Saint Bernard than a sophisticated man. She was helping him recover from his loss, and that was helpful to her, too. That's all, she insisted.

Still, they both needed companionship, and they were comfortable together. They were becoming best friends. The relationship was less one sided these days. Andy was able to hear more of Carole's memories and sadness, have her spin her hopes and dreams. He was also more able to share the concerns of her day-to day-living. They watched movies, talked about current events, and shared laughter.

These days, Andy worked more efficiently. He made progress refurbishing the motel, and smiling, he told Carole of his plans to name rooms after his family. It gave his work meaning.

New Terrain

D.A. Reilly checked in on Andy every week or two, asking how he was doing and if he needed anything. Now, the time had come to begin the preparation for the trial, a trial they expected would happen that fall. They would have a series of face-to-face meetings over the next few months as the D.A.'s office put their case together. The initial meeting related to trial preparation focused on the logistics, the location, the roles of various people involved, the rules for testimony, and the support systems in place for the family to use. Reilly reminded Andy that the support group was one of those resources. The process of preparation was intentionally spread out because of the emotional intensity of the work and because it allowed more time to consider how the case would be presented.

Having to think about the case, the murder scene, LaPlante himself, and the media resurfaced for Andy an inner turmoil that had only recently begun to decrease a bit. But he now had more resources—time with family and friends, Carole's companionship, the grief support group, and his spiritual walks, locally and away. He flew to the Vineyard anytime the weather was good and the plane was available. It was a beautiful time of year by the ocean.

His desire to have a place on this island year-round grew strong. He had been checking out the properties listed in the newspaper and posted on the windows of real estate offices. Finally, he set up an appointment and met with a real estate agent to investigate available properties. He collected the options and described them, one by one, with Carole one night soon after that visit. He was particularly drawn to a cottage at the Methodist Campgrounds in Oak Bluffs. This historic village of summer cottages with roots in the nineteenth century Methodist camp movement still hosted interdenominational worship services and Bible studies. One cottage had caught his eye, a two-story narrow house with a front porch big enough for two rocking chairs, a screened side porch, and a small deck off a second story window. Its price, though a stretch, was possible, and it ignited Andy's imagination.

Andy invited Carole to fly to the Vineyard with him to see the property. Andy's flying skills were only slightly better than his driving, and he clipped some of the runway lights as he landed, more than a bit scary for Carole; but once she saw the cottage, she smiled. She loved the porches and the gingerbread filigree that characterized the little encampment. Although the Tabernacle offered worship only during July and August, she could feel the values and life of the community that would come to full bloom in the summer. Her experience studying real estate allowed her to explain the complexities of buying an easement rather than getting a deed outright. The association owned the land and there would be many rules. This would not be a simple transaction, whether buying, selling, or maintaining. On the other hand, there would be people who would be eager to rent, and reselling the easement, when the time came, would be painless, as there was good demand for moderately priced housing on the island, she thought. They discussed the offer Andy proposed and submitted it. After some back and forth negotiation, the seller accepted the offer, and they waited for the lawyers and the board of the community to complete the necessary steps.

That week at the support group, Andy talked about how his time on the Vineyard was one of the ways he coped and found peace. He shared how walking was his time to pray and pour out his emotions to God. It also provided the opportunity to restart a practice he had learned long ago from Cilla—to think about people and places in his life today for which he was grateful. "Sometimes," he told them, "I repeat Bible verses again and again. One of the more important ones is from the book of John. I even wrote it on the tombstone: The Light shines in the darkness and the darkness cannot over come it."

Andy's sister Karen came from Amherst regularly to hang out with her little brother. They shared good family memories as they grieved. One night that spring, Andy mentioned that he and Cilla had begun planning a trip to England, taking books out of the library, discussing the history, and staring at pictures. They imagined visits to the Tower of London, Buckingham Palace, Big Ben, and Westminster Abby.

"Let's go," Karen offered impulsively. "Let's you and I do that trip. You bring Cilla in your heart and share it with her that way. I've always wanted to explore England, too."

In May, they flew to London, traveling around for about a week. Off U.S. soil, laughter came more easily. They both talked to Cilla aloud as if she were with them, pointing out the sites, recounting history and making up responses she would have had. This was a new way to carry his love with him.

Returning from England, Andy learned of the legal tangles that ensnarled the Vineyard transaction. Motivated by personal goals, Andy applied his real estate finesse, cleared the multiple hurdles, finished the documents, notified all parties, oversaw bank transfers, and gathered the required signatures. Closed.

The experience of the legal work connected to the Vineyard was eye opening. When he was motivated, when his work aligned with his values, he was able to concentrate on his work and access the skills and abilities that were present before the murder. He had worried he would never be able to work effectively again, that somehow his brain had been damaged by the trauma. But, no. He had been a great lawyer in this transaction. This felt very hopeful, a fact he celebrated with Carole. But it also raised the questions he had intermittently raised before. What kind of legal work might I do that would let this kind of energy flow again? Clearly, his values mattered. Clearly the purpose of the work being done needed to align with something important.

Tales of Terror

As the trial grew closer, Andy obsessed about Daniel LaPlante and how it would feel to be in the same room with him. Andy had heard bizarre anecdotes about Daniel's behavior at school and on playgrounds. Most disturbing was the tale people called the prequel to the Gustafson murders. These crimes were the charges that were pending when Daniel was bailed out by his mother in October. Yet the story was so intense it would haunt the dreams of people who heard the tale. Andy decided he needed to bring this story to the grief support group in an attempt not to be paralyzed by the images, especially as he prepared to testify.

When LaPlante was about sixteen, he and a girl from a neighboring town dated for a short while. The girl's mother had recently died and she needed to feel loved and cared for. Initially intrigued by this suave, charming, good-looking young man, it took only a couple of weeks before she felt uncomfortable around him and broke up the relationship. The girl supported her dad in caring for her two younger sisters, all of them trying to cope with the loss. About two weeks after the break up, she was babysitting for her sisters and watching a movie. The girls started to notice weird things—snacks disappearing from the kitchen, some strange, unexplained sounds—but they discounted them.

The eight-year-old was going off to bed as the dad arrived home. She opened her closet to discover LaPlante, dressed in her dead mother's clothes, his face smeared with make-up (some reports called it face paint), and brandishing a hatchet. He whispered, "Be quiet or I'll kill you." LaPlante tied up the terrified eight-year-old. He then accosted the rest of the family, including the father, tying them up, and taunting them with the hatchet. "Do you know how to pray? Huh? You better pray now because I'm coming back to kill you, in just a few minutes." As he rummaged through drawers and shelves looking for valuables, the youngest child wriggled free, jumped out the window, and ran to the neighbors, who called the police. Grabbing his gun, the neighbor rushed next door, found the family, untied them, but did not find LaPlante. When the police arrived, they searched the house and the grounds thoroughly, to no avail. The police advised the family to leave for a while.

The family vacated the house for two weeks. LaPlante remained on the loose. When the family pulled into the driveway after their two-week absence, there was LaPlante, standing in the window. The father screamed, and the neighbor responded, calling 911 and joining the father in watching the exits until the police arrived. Law enforcement searched, and could not locate the youth. They were, however, alarmed by what they did find: walls covered with strange writing, and pennies glued to the ceiling. They combed each room in the house, peering in closets and looking under beds. Nothing. They switched on the lights in the basement, rummaged among the boxes, and found nothing. Then, they heard a noise coming from behind the washing machine. Pulling the washer away from the wall, they found a hole. In that hole was Daniel LaPlante. It was then they realized, there were holes in many places, peepholes. It appeared that LaPlante had been living in the walls of the family house.

Andy stumbled through his version of the story, shaking and crying. People shook their heads and mumbled, "That's so hard to believe." "Terrifying." "He must be a psychopath."

Andy recomposed himself and spun out his anger, his questions, his rage. "LaPlante has been in and out of juvenile facilities for serious crimes. He gets out after a little more than a year, and bang, within a short time, he is charged with this bizarre home invasion. They lock him up awaiting trial, and then they allow his mother to bail him out. Why did they release him on bail? Did they not recognize who he was? Are there no laws and psychological services that recognize the danger? Less than a month out on bail, he starts a robbery spree, including our house. It was like he stalked us. Why did he choose my beautiful wife and my young children? Was it the swing set in the back yard? Had he seen Cilla around town, at the drug store where she worked, or at a church event? Or was it random? I don't know. Evidently during the break in, he found her keys, and hid them near the house. That's how he got in, without forced entry. He had keys—keys that we didn't recognize had been taken. Damn our messiness."

The leader addressed the guilt. "These murders are not your fault. I am so sorry you are having to endure such torture."

"He tortured my family. Tortured my beautiful children, and I can't even think about what he did to my wife. How can he be human? He is evil incarnate. And our legal system failed us. Our psychological system failed. It failed, and my family paid the cost."

The group mourned together, sharing their compassion and their wisdom.

As the evening drew to a close, the leader had the group circle around Andy. "If you feel comfortable doing so," the leader guided, "I invite you to repeat these phrases, lines that Andy has told us are helpful to him. They are helpful to me, too, right now. 'The light shines in the darkness, and the darkness has not overcome it.'"

The group repeated, "The light shines in the darkness, and the darkness has not overcome it." The chant became one, a community voice, that built and held the circle.

Then the leader shifted to, "A Love that is stronger than death." The group responded, "A Love that is stronger than death." The group shared the Love that had grown among them, a Love that was stronger than the horrific story, a Love that rooted Andy in his faith.

It took longer than usual for the group to disband that night. Arriving home, Andy could not sleep. He drove over to the cemetery and stood with his family, shaking, crying, praying, until finally, he found a peace he couldn't explain. It was as if the angels of his family came to minister to him.

A few days later, Andy flew to the Vineyard to touch the peace he found in that place. As he looked at the gingerbread decorations on the front of many houses in the encampment, an idea struck him. He would create carvings of angels for the railing of the cottage. He would return to working in wood, focusing his mind and his hands on creativity, a creativity that integrated Cilla and the children into his new life, constantly reminding him that they were angels, close at hand. This would be Angel Cottage, a place where he could pray in the way Cilla had taught him, a place where he could walk the beaches the way he had with his children, a place where he could read, think, and worship, disconnected from the notoriety, the horror, and the pain of Townsend.

Andy recognized a deepening spiritual wisdom and a connection to things unseen. His dreams were vivid and sometimes comforting.

Angel Cottage at Oakbluff, MA. Notice the carvings on the second floor balcony and on the roof line. Picture, circa 2012, posted on Facebook.

Separately, Cilla, Abby, and Billy sent messages like, "I love you," and "We are with God." Andy woke from these encounters with a warmth and groundedness he described as "the peace that passes understanding." As spring turned to summer, Cilla came to Andy in his dreams again, encouraging him to keep on living, giving him permission to choose life, promising they were angels watching over him that would not leave him.

The cottage became his home away from home. Sometimes he brought Carole, sometimes other friends or family, sometimes he came on his own. During the summer, he would go to the movies, listen to guest preachers, attend band concerts, and sing in his loud, off-key voice without being noticed. Here, he smiled often and began to feel joy.

A Surprising Turn

The friendship between Carole and Andy deepened into an intimacy of sharing their innermost thoughts, emotions, and dreams, but it was still platonic. They would hold hands to offer support when emotions got tough, hug each other in deep caring, greet one another, and say good night warmly, but this was not a dating relationship. They were two adults companioning one another through grief—nothing more, nothing less.

Then one July night, something surprising happened. Perhaps there had been too much Jim Beam flowing, perhaps it was the movie they watched, perhaps it was the encouragement of Cilla in his dreams, but Andy initiated a change in their relationship.

Carole smiles in the remembering, her eyes gazing upward. "It felt good for both of us. We had been lonely and alone for so long. It was spontaneous, an unexpected surprise, that first kiss. Andy pulled me close and I melted into his arms. It all flowed from there. The next morning, or a perhaps it was a few days later, the neighbor across the street from my house on the common stopped me with a chuckle.

"'Didn't I see Andy's car in your drive way at five a.m.? Overnight, huh?'

"I blushed a little, I think, and mumbled, 'He sometimes sleeps on my couch.' But I think I was glowing in a way that was new."

Carole, so fearless in being present in the depths of despondency that was Andy's emotional default, so drawn to his spiritual depth, now added the giddiness of romantic love to the mix. It was like another twirl on the roller coaster. They were a couple.

That evening shifted the conversation between Carole and Andy from the past–present to the present–future. The level of honesty and intimacy allowed them to name the doubts and conflicts they had about each other, as well as claim the deep love that had developed between them. Each of them knew that their first loves, Cilla for Andy and Greg for Carole, would remain important and present in their consciousness forever. They both had made life-long commitments and given their whole selves in these first marriages, these relationships of young love, chemistry, and promise. But they were different now. Having been tempered by anguish and suffering, both had an appreciation of the preciousness of each day, an awareness of the amazing gift of living on earth, a gratitude for the blessings that surrounded them in family, in God's creation, in their community of faith.

By mid-summer the trial preparation was in full swing. Andy met regularly with prosecutors from the D.A.'s office. The D.A.'s lawyers reviewed the procedural motions under consideration. Unless the defense won one of its motions, the trial would be at the Lowell Court house. Andy was familiar with that location. Trial preparation focused on telling and retelling the story of December first. They needed to figure out the sequence, the words that would work, the details that needed to be remembered, the order that would make sense to the jury. He needed to rehearse enough to be able to be adequately composed, to develop coping mechanisms to deal with LaPlante's presence in the room, to be able to manage cross-examination without emotionally disintegrating. This was a time to practice.

One evening in the support group, the meeting began with a time focused on trials and trial preparation. Group members shared different approaches to managing trials. Some wanted to be present at every session. Others came only when they testified. Some started with one strategy and shifted to another as the trial proceeded. "Don't look at the perpetrator," advised one member. "Look at the attorney who is questioning you. Look at the jury. Lock onto people in the courtroom who give you strength and love."

When Andy and Cilla's family gathered, they too talked about preparing for the trial. "I want justice! I want to look that man in the face and tell him what he destroyed!" cried Christine.

Andy supported her. "I want you to do what is best for you. I may make a different choice. I don't think I'll attend the trial, except when I have to be there, and I don't want to even look at LaPlante. I hope that's all right with you. I hope you will not feel unsupported by me."

They nodded their understanding. "Do what is best for you."

Later Carole asked, "Do you want me to go with you to court?"

"No." He paused. "I don't think either of us needs to give this man any more recognition than he already is getting in the media. And I do not believe it will help me heal. Likely, it would only pour vinegar in my wounds."

And so it was decided.

Andy and Carole made intentional efforts to build a boundary between their life and the court and not to let the trial consume precious time and energy. They wanted to foster this love growing between them and to let it shine among their friends and family. Andy brought Carole on the Gustafson family camping trip to the Saco River, which had been a summer highlight for Cilla and the children. It was a big step. Carole had met his family—his sister Karen, his brother Larry and wife Shelley, and his parents Shirley and Leonard––but now she claimed a different role. She felt awkward coming into a routine that this crew knew by heart. Camping was Andy's joy, as it had been since his boyhood Scouting days.

The Saco River, with its white sandy shores and clear stream, offered opportunities to canoe, kayak, and tube. The group relaxed around the evening campfires, sharing laughter and memories, enjoying libations and roasted marshmallows. Little by little, Carole did too.

Summer waned. September brought beautiful blue skies, flashes of red and yellow leaves, and a sense of change in the air. Carole and Andy sat together at church and went to social functions as a couple. But even with this shift in relationship, Andy struggled with his grief, often waking in the night, wailing the ache in his soul, missing the children's voices, longing for Cilla's touch, haunted by the reality of the violence. This kind of wailing rips at listeners who feel helpless in the face of such agony. And so it was for Carole. In such times, all she could do was hold him, pray for him, do what she could to stay present when he touched the shattered place he carried. Still, it was when Andy was alone that the greatest intensity of grief would engulf him. But he was getting better. The breakdowns didn't happen every time he went to sleep, and he didn't wake up in the middle of every night. Gradually the frequency decreased and the intensity dissipated, but it was years before it was not a regular occurrence. Carole's acceptance of this part of Andy was a significant gift and a bond of love between them.

Andy and Carole talked of marriage, even though it had been only ten months since the murders. To some, this seemed unwise, but both Andy and Carole knew that life was short, unpredictable, and precious. They decided they didn't need the approval of others if it was clear to them. But they would not set a date until the trial, scheduled to begin at the end of the month, was complete.

The Trial Opens,
The Stage Is Set

September brought pretrial motions, and the renewed barrage of media attention on Townsend and the murders of the Gustafson family. Robert Sheketoff and David Duncan, now LaPlante's defense team, requested that the previous convictions for robbery and sexual assault not be mentioned during the murder trial. The judge agreed. The defense asked to block the admittance of four letters LaPlante wrote while in prison, bragging to a cell-mate of his crimes. Since that inmate had asked "for considerations" when he brought the incriminating letters forward, the judge granted their request to have them banned.[5] The defense team petitioned to have the case moved out of eastern Massachusetts, because of all the publicity, contending that it would be hard to find an impartial jury. This brought an emotional volley from the judge: "Mr. LaPlante will be tried in Lowell, and in this court."[6] The defense proffered an alternative; have the jury chosen from a different area. The judge considered this proposal overnight and granted it the next day. The jury would be chosen from a pool in western Massachusetts.

Monday, October 3, 1988, the attorneys in the LaPlante trial traveled to the Springfield Court to select a jury, seeking people who had not heard much about this case. They selected five on

Monday and eleven more on Tuesday.[7] Stating that the case before them would be complex and probably drawn out, the judge requested that the jurors return the next day packed for several weeks away from home. They would be sequestered, stay at a local hotel, be transported to court each day by bus, and have all their phone calls and visits monitored to ensure they had no access to news media. Their expenses would be covered by the court, including laundry services, meals, and basic needs.

Wednesday, the selected jurors and alternates settled into their temporary rooms in Lowell. They began the task of getting to know each other and building mutual trust. With the guidance of court assistants, they elected jury officers.

Thursday morning, October sixth, the bus picked up the jurors at the hotel at about nine and brought them to the side door of the Lowell courthouse, as would be the practice for the next three weeks. The brick-and-marble municipal building had limited public parking, with the media required to leave their vehicles in private lots on adjacent streets. Dozens of reporters and photographers stood on the courthouse steps each day, thirsty for the attention-grabbing news their bosses coveted, in hopes of boosting ratings. Only a few journalists were allowed in the courtroom itself, having been instructed to share their notes with the media pool. Inside the building, up one flight of marble stairs, down a long, echoing hallway and through heavy wooden doors, sat the Superior Court, a square room with three high windows, a marble floor, twelve-foot walls, and a few framed pictures of current officials in Massachusetts and Washington D.C. General seating offered a few rows of hard benches.

Most days, Cilla's sisters arrived at the proceedings early to ensure a place. The guard at the door, soon recognizing them, surreptitiously saved them seats if they were late by steering other visitors elsewhere. When empty, as it usually was when the sisters arrived, the courtroom echoed, but when all the benches were full, the acoustics improved. A large, raised desk of polished oak built across the front of the room contained the judge's bench, marked by a black rolling chair. To its right was the witness stand with a wooden railing and microphone, and behind on either side were the Massachusetts and U.S. flags. To either side of the bench stood the bailiff and the uniformed state police officer assigned to the court. Tucked under the bench, the stenographer recorded the proceedings, silent except for the clicking of the keys on her machine. The prosecutors and defense lawyers, sitting at separate tables, faced the bench, a microphone podium available at each location.

At 10 a.m., the court officer closed the gallery door to additional observers, requiring latecomers to seek the guard's permission to enter thereafter. It was then that the police officers escorted into the courtroom the defendant, a good-looking youth of medium stature and slight build, with light brown stylized hair slicked to stand on end. The shackles on his feet clanked as he walked, but with his hands free and his street clothes neatly ironed, he looked respectable sitting at the table. At about 10:05 the bailiff signaled, "All rise." Everyone did, with LaPlante the last to get up, his reluctance, the hint of a sneer, his slouch already communicating disregard for the process despite the original impression. Some there caught LaPlante's eye-roll as the bailiff intoned, "The Honorable Robert A. Barton, Chief Magistrate of the Middlesex Superior Court, presiding." The judge sat and the bailiff indicated that everyone could do likewise.

On the judge's signal, the twelve jurors, seven women and five men, as well as the four alternates filed into the courtroom, sitting to the right of the bench, with a good view of the witness box and the defendant with his lawyers. After a brief pause as the jurors settled into their places, putting the few things they were allowed to bring into court in appropriate places, the judge greeted them. He asked whether they had any needs to present to the court, and then proceeded to give them a legal overview of the trial. He reminded them that more specific instructions would be given whenever needed, and that they were invited to communicate any questions for the judge through the foreman or the assistant foreman. The judge then turned toward the lawyers, looked directly at the defendant, and requested that he rise. LaPlante complied. The judge read an abbreviated version of the indictment.

"Do you understand these charges?" the judge asked.

LaPlante nodded.

"How do you plead?"

"Not guilty," LaPlante said loudly.

The Judge continued, "In our country, defendants are judged by a jury of their peers, with the prosecution presenting a case in the affirmative, and the defense carefully attending to the rights and interests of the defendant. The defendant may be seated."

Turning to Assistant District Attorney Thomas Reilly, Barton instructed, "Please present your opening arguments, beginning with the prosecution."

Reilly stood and spoke, his voice strong and emotional, laying out the essential elements of his case, and giving an overview of the witnesses who would be called. When Reilly sat, the judge turned to the court-appointed defense attorney, Robert Sheketoff. "Your opening statement?"

Sheketoff replied, "The defense declines to make an opening statement." The collective breath of surprise echoed in the court, many there shocked, since the media had reported that Sheketoff contended the case was circumstantial and there were other possible suspects. But the defense made no such argument where it counted. People expected the attorneys were deferring their best case for later.

The judge gestured for the prosecution to begin. During pretrial negotiations, Reilly proposed a guided tour of the crime sites, giving the jury a context for testimony, having them experience the places and the relationships among different locations that would be crucial to understanding the testimony. That was today's plan. The judge directed the defendant be returned to his cell, while the jurors, the judge, the attorneys, several court officers and the lead investigators boarded a bus to travel the thirty miles to West Townsend where they would see the places that would be central to the upcoming testimony. A handful of media shadowed the day's tour.

Arriving in Townsend, the bus turned off Route 119 onto Saunders Road, the sign "dead end" posted at its entry. Up the hill and around the corner, they came to a dirt driveway, more than one hundred yards long, bridging a gully full of trees. The house was secluded, but visible from the road, set on a small knoll. The bus did not negotiate the long driveway, instead discharging the passengers to walk. The brown two-story house with a central door was in good repair, the small area of grass mowed, the stone stairs sturdy and aligned. A sticker that firefighters use to locate children's rooms marked one of the second floor windows. Once inside, the jurors walked from room to room—the entry hallway, the kitchen, the downstairs bath, the stairway, the master bedroom, the children's rooms and the upstairs bath.

An investigator guided the observations. "You might pay attention to the size of the rooms, the layout of the house and the distance between rooms....Notice what is visible from different locations and/or out of view in another....Move around as makes sense to you...Some jurors find it useful to consider the placement of windows, how doors open and close, the width and relative angles of the stairway....Take notes, if that helps, or you can ask a court officer to assist you with that if you like."

The jury spent extra time in the master bedroom, considering the location of the closet, the way the various doors moved, the type and placement of the bedroom set. What they were seeing would help them visualize the events, as witnesses recalled stories of the victims, the perpetrator, the husband and the investigators. The jurors asked questions, took notes, stopped to study different rooms, shifted to see different perspectives. "Have you had enough time?" the judge asked. The jurors nodded.

The next phase was outdoors. The investigator pointed to the location of the sneaker footprint, the placement from which the Gustafsons' nameplate was stolen and later recovered, and the unlikely spot where officers found Priscilla's keys, over the embankment, under some branches. As the jurors continued toward the path in the woods, they passed the children's swing set and a stand of red and yellow maples. After a short walk that crossed a stream in the next gully, the officer stopped, pointing to a stake in the ground. "That's where we located the checkered shirt, the soaked gloves and the nameplate, items that will be introduced into evidence later in the trial." Some of the jurors knelt to get a closer look, others scanned to determine the distance from the Gustafsons' house to the road ahead of them. Continuing through the woods, a juror accepted the arm of court officer as the brush obscured a real path and required balance to negotiate. This was not a frequently traveled trail.

The crowd arrived at the defendant's residence, noting that both the porch and the house needed repairs. A court officer cautioned people to walk carefully around scattered tools, discarded appliances and non-functioning cars. The court group did not enter LaPlante's house, but walked to the backyard, to view the Jeep Cherokee where a family member discovered the murder weapon. The officer leaned in to open the glove compartment.

The judge, recognizing some people's struggle with mobility and stamina, offered the choice of walking or riding to the next site. From the back of LaPlante's house, it was less than a mile to the next destination, but the path crossed the town line into Pepperell. It took the bus almost as long to get to the small development as it did for the people going through the woods. Here, during the manhunt, LaPlante tried to enter several houses. Here, LaPlante hid in the woods, confronted the sixteen year old, and made her drive him toward Fitchburg. The jury learned the proximity of the various sites and realized how easily LaPlante could have traveled across the town line, hiding in the underbrush for more than a day.

There was one more part of the excursion. Boarding the bus, they retraced the route taken by the orange escape van, driven initially by the sixteen year old Makela and ultimately by defendant LaPlante. The investigator pointed out the stop light where Makela escaped, the parking lot where LaPlante abandoned the van and the lumberyard dumpster in Ayer where the police apprehended the suspect. As the sunlight began to fade, the judge stood at the front of the bus, took a deep breath, smiled his appreciation at those in front of him and spoke.

"Today's time in the field has given you a context for hearing the testimony. I know this has been a long, physically challenging day. We, the people, thank you for your service to the Commonwealth. Remember the restrictions required by sequestration that I have explained, but also take some time to relax. The next days will require your full attention."

Testimony Begins

The next day the trial began in earnest. Before the judge was seated, Andy Gustafson slipped into the gallery and sat with his sisters-in-law. Andy would be in the courtroom only two times, this day and the last. Carole decided, in conversation with Andy, that she would never attend.

The first witness, a nine-year-old girl, Abby's neighbor and friend, rode home on the school bus with her that day. Seeing this child walk from the adjoining room to the witness box, a little girl about the same age as Abby, barely able to see over the railing, was a subtle but emotional reminder of the murdered children. Reilly asked simple questions—about that Tuesday, the bus ride, the walk home, going out to play.

"Did you hear something?"

"I heard a scream and a dog barking."

"How long was the scream?"

"About fifteen seconds."

"Where were you when you heard the scream?"

"In the back of the house, down the hill a little."

"Where was the scream coming from?"

"From Abby's house."

"Could you tell if it was a boy or a girl screaming?"

"It was a girl's scream."[8]

There were some muffled gasps and sobs from the courtroom.

"Thank you," concluded Reilly.

"Any cross-examination from the defense?" the judge asked.

"None," came the reply.

"Then you are excused. Thank you."

Andy knew that he was the second witness for the prosecution. He breathed deeply, struggling to maintain his composure. The bailiff called, "Andrew Gustafson." This would be the first time he had spoken publicly since the funeral.

Now thirty-four, his strawberry blond hairline receding, his hands fiddling nervously, Andy walked forward, averting his eyes to avoid looking at the defendant. He knew this would be difficult, despite the hours of preparation with D.A. Tom Reilly. He took the oath, fixing his eyes on the prosecutor, breathing with intention. Step by step, Reilly led him through the basic information: his address, line of work, relationship to the victims, and a description of the home.

Carefully, gently, Reilly questioned Andy, guiding him to retrace the events, starting with the November robbery, then on to the events of December first. Andy maintained his composure, pushing his glasses up on his face several times, choosing his words carefully.[9]

But he shifted in his seat, his body jerked and his voice cracked as he told about his three unanswered phone calls, the drive home, and finding Cilla's maroon van parked and the house dark. By now, he had crossed his arms and was clutching himself in a hug, subtly rocking back and forth, laboring to talk loud enough for the jury to hear.

In almost a whisper, Reilly encouraged him to continue.

Andy began to cry, his words coming out in bursts as he recalled phoning the babysitter, climbing the stairs, opening the bedroom door. In the court room, he cried out and covered his face.

Reilly paused for a few seconds, took a breath and then coached Andy,

"Breathe. . . . Look at me."

It took part of a minute, but Andy did.

"Can you go on?" Reilly asked. Andy nodded.

"How did you know she was dead?" Reilly queried.

"She was lifeless. Her hands and feet had that gray pallor of death."

"And then."

Andy seemed paralyzed for a few seconds before he continued.

"I went to the kitchen to call 911, and my parents." Andy took an audible breath. "Then I decided I had to go up one more time."

The jurors could see the small movements as he replayed those moments in his mind's eye, then a gasp and a sob, "That's when I saw the bullet holes." He moaned slightly. "I did not look further." He stuttered, "I... I was afraid to find the children dead." His face was in his hands.

The D.A. waited. In the courtroom, some held their breath, some cried with Andy, others stared down at the floor. Reilly reached out in support as Andy again regained some composure.

"Do you need a break?" asked the judge.

Andy shook his head no.

Reilly asked a few more questions, and then announced the end of his examination. The judge gestured for the defense to cross-examine. Instead, the defense attorney replied, "No questions at this time."

The judge dismissed Andy, who left the courtroom not to return until the day the judgment would be handed down, and ordered a twenty-minute recess. The jury filed out for a needed break, while Cilla's sisters held each other and sobbed.

When the court reconvened, Patrolman John W. Johns, the first officer to respond, took the stand. He recounted responding to the 911 call at the Saunders Road home and finding the husband, Andy, despondent. After Sergeant Irving Marshall arrived,

Johns reported that he searched the house, found William in the upstairs bathroom, face down in a dry tub, his body neatly clothed, and Abby in the downstairs bathroom tub, in four inches of water. Her skin and clothes showed signs of a struggle. The jury saw the evidence photos taken that day.

Townsend Chief of Police Bill May testified next, reviewing and expanding the story Andy told. He described the gathering of evidence including the interview that led him to conclude that Andrew Gustafson was not a suspect.

After several hours of testimony, Reilly led May to explain how the murder weapon was found. May testified that the December searches of the LaPlante house had found ammunition of the caliber and type that killed Priscilla Gustafson, but had not discovered the murder weapon. Months later, on April 7 at 2:00 a.m., May responded to a call from the LaPlante residence. "I met Elaine Moore, Daniel's mother, her husband David, and Daniel's attorney, Robert Casey, at 22 West Elm Street," May testified. "Brother Steven had found a suspicious gun. Together, we went to the Jeep Cherokee parked behind the house. Inside the glove compartment, we found a pistol, a holster and belt, and the .22 caliber revolver later identified as the murder weapon. Two guns had been stolen from a neighbor, Raymond Bindell, but no ammunition was taken." Bindell would later attest to the October 14, 1987, robbery, but assert that only two guns were taken. The ammunition, which he kept in another part of the house, was untouched. Witnesses for the prosecution would trace LaPlante's efforts to buy ammunition.

The Defense team did not cross-examine these witnesses.

Defensiveness with No Defense

Brightly-colored leaves were set against blue skies as court reconvened the following week. State Trooper Stephen Matthews, dressed in his uniform, tall shiny boots, and his most professional manner, began the day's testimony reviewing the initial investigation: searching the Gustafsons' house for evidence, questioning motorists in a road block on Route 119, canvassing the neighbors door to door, creating a list of people to be investigated. LaPlante, a teen out on bail, was on that list. He recounted the interview with LaPlante at the library and the later attempt to arrest Daniel that launched the manhunt.

The next person called to the stand was Daniel's brother, Stephen. His testimony told of his encounter with the police who were searching for his brother, and the beginning of the manhunt. Then the prosecutor continued, "Stephen, tell us about the ammunition and the .22 caliber gun."

Stephen spoke. "After Danny got bailed out last October, he kept asking me and all our friends for bullets. He would tell us that he wanted to make a big bullet out of small ones. I know that sounds strange, but that's just how Danny thinks, not quite like other people."

"And the gun, Stephen? You found the gun?"

"Oh, that was months later. Michael and I were out in the

junky Jeep in the back yard. I don't know exactly why I opened the glove compartment, but I did, and to my surprise, there was a gun, one I hadn't seen before. I didn't touch it, I told my parents. They called the lawyer, even though it was pretty late. He's the one that called the cops. I think it was the middle of the night when we all met up at the Jeep. Creepy."

Again, the defense asked no follow-up questions.

The last two witnesses of the day were the dog-tracking officers who had found the shirt in the woods that led them to LaPlante's house. Another day in court ended, with Cilla's sisters exhausted but determined to continue the vigil. They wanted to confront LaPlante directly, to look into his eyes, to tell him the devastation he had brought to their family. Today was not that day.

The next two days, Daniel's mother Elaine and stepfather David testified. Elaine took the stand armored for the encounter-- her face steeled, her words edgy, her voice shrill. She was a mother bear protecting her young. The testimony that started off benign quickly escalated to a heated exchange marked by abrasive, rapid-paced volleys, culminating in accusations focused on the blue tartan pattern shirt discarded in the woods, the one with bloodstains.

"Did the shirt belong to your husband?"

"Was it borrowed by Daniel?"

Elaine Moore had answered those questions multiple times before: during the initial police interviews on December 2, at the grand jury, and during this trial. Did she identify the shirt or not? Her answers didn't match up. Even on the witness stand, she was self-contradictory, insisting she had told the truth to the grand jury, complaining she felt threatened by the district attorney's warning, "if you lied about it, you'll go to jail." The attorney, agitated, and moving toward the witness box, accused, "You're lying. It can't be both ways. Is it your husband's shirt or not? Did Daniel wear it or not?"

With the argument heated and a clear resolution improbable, Judge Barton intervened, stopping this line of questioning, trying to de-escalate the interchange by acknowledging that there were multiple stories. But Reilly continued, prodding Moore to identify Daniel's biological father, seeking to corroborate rumors repeated around Townsend. Moore, almost baring her teeth, snorted, "How dare you? I will not."

"Enough!" silenced the Judge. "Let her have her privacy. It is not relevant to this case."

The following day David Moore, Daniel's stepfather, took the stand. After the perfunctory opening questions, the focus turned to events in mid-November. While sorting laundry, Moore discovered a .22 caliber revolver among Daniel's clothes.

"What did you do?" queried Reilly.

"I put the gun in Daniel's face and asked him where he got it."

"Asked? Really?" Reilly challenged.

"No, I yelled at him."

At the defense table, Daniel crossed his arms, dropped his head, and slipped lower in his chair.

"And what next?" continued Reilly.

"Daniel said, 'Chill.'" Moore gestured, with both palms up. "He said he'd gotten the gun last year, bought it from a guy in Westminster. He told me that it had been in the house for a year."

"So, what did you do?" Reilly pressed.

"I asked if there was anything else in the house that I should know about." His voice communicated disdain.

"And was there?"

"Daniel said, 'Nothing,'" Moore shrugged. "I told him I was taking the gun and putting it in my tool chest at the machine shop in Groton."

"Did you call the police? Daniel was out on bail, right?"

Moore shook his head and looked down. "No, I didn't."

"So, what did you do to him?" the questioning continued.

"Do to him? Nothing, really."

"Nothing? Really?"

Exasperated, Moore said, "Well we screamed and hollered at him. We warned him that he could get in big trouble."

Reilly, "But no call to the police, or his juvenile officer."

Moore, quieter now, "No."

Reilly pushed on. "Did you search his room or look through the rest of the house to see if you'd find other things, to verify what Daniel was saying?"

Moore, much softer, "No, didn't do that."

Reilly, "The gun was in Groton until when?"

Moore continued, "After the cops arrested Daniel, and I realized they were following me, I gave the gun to my brother, asked him to hold it. He never asked me about the gun and I never told him."

Later testimony revealed that the gun David Moore hid and the gun that was used in the murder had both been stolen from a neighbor, Raymond Bindell, on October 14, 1987, a few days after Daniel was released on bail.

The defense declined to cross-examine, but did make a motion requesting that the judge instruct the jury to consider whether someone who committed such a crime was sane. Judge Barton, with a thoughtful look, said he would take this motion under advisement. Although psychiatric teams had observed LaPlante at Bridgewater State Hospital soon after his arrest, it was unclear at that point whether the defense had evidence to plead an insanity defense.

Michael H. Polowski Jr., twenty-four, a frequent visitor to the LaPlante household, was called to the stand. He testified that Daniel LaPlante had asked him repeatedly for ammunition. After stalling for several weeks, Polowski gave him some in late November. "I gave him some with a warning," Michael asserted. "I told him not to do anything harmful."

"Where did you get the ammunition?" the prosecutor asked.

"From a man I knew as Mark, in Fitchburg. He'd offered to sell me a .22 caliber rifle with a telescopic sight for sixty-five dollars. I suspected it was stolen goods, but I decided to take it anyway."

The defense team, or perhaps LaPlante himself, began to create an alternative scenario—that Michael Polowski was a likely suspect who could have committed all of the murders. The defense team wondered aloud whether the police had considered him, looked at his whereabouts, sampled his DNA. But that scenario wouldn't be used now because the defense team hadn't developed the evidence that would be needed to present that argument. That scenario was presented in the appeal.

The prosecution called Pamela Makela, the young woman held at gunpoint who drove the get-away car during the manhunt, and heard her emotional story. Then a stream of witnesses testified about the forensic evidence and the autopsies. The evidence mounted.

Finally the prosecution rested its case. All eyes turned to the defense. To everyone's surprise, the defense rested—with no opening or closing statements, without cross examining anyone, without calling a single witness, not even psychiatrists from Bridgewater State Hospital where LaPlante had spent almost a month for observation and testing. They had made many procedural motions, but offered no affirmative defense. Were they making an opening for an appeal?

Judge Barton addressed the eighteen-year-old defendant. "Do you, young man, wish to speak on your own behalf?" LaPlante shook his head. The judge then declared, "Final arguments will be presented next Monday. The jury can be expected to begin their deliberations by early afternoon."

The jury stayed in Lowell for another weekend of sequestered living. Monday morning, October 24, three weeks into the trial, the prosecution presented final arguments and summarized the key evidence presented by the 49 witnesses and the 224 exhibits. They argued that the motive for the crime was probably robbery, but that these murders were irrational, heinous. The defense made no closing arguments, the silence putting the burden of proof on the prosecution. The judge instructed the jury in the legal requirements of the task ahead and sent them to deliberate. They met for three hours on Monday and reconvened the next day. Late Tuesday morning, the jury signaled that they had made a decision.

The court convened at two o'clock in the afternoon, with Andy Gustafson and Cilla's two sisters, Christine and Beth, present. The Judge turned to the jury. "Have you reached a verdict, Mr. Foreman?"

James Fallon responded, "Yes sir, we have," and handed the bailiff a note, which the Judge read and returned.

"How say you?" asked the judge, following the ritual.

"We find the defendant guilty on all charges."

LaPlante, still seated at the defense table, drummed his interlaced fingers and smirked. Judge Barton, furious at LaPlante's actions, bellowed at the defendant, "Mr. LaPlante, you will stand and face your country!"

With an arrogant squirm and an even broader smirk, the teen complied.

Assistant D.A. Reilly was passionate. "Never in my experience have I seen such a heinous crime. The defendant has never shown the slightest bit of remorse for the people who died because they got in his way. We ask the court to impose three consecutive life sentences, with no parole."

The Judge turned to the defense. "What say you?" he asked.

Sheketoff replied with little emotion, "We ask that the sentences be concurrent, since this is life without parole. After all, Judge, LaPlante was only seventeen at the time of the crime, a juvenile."

Judge Barton was clear as he addressed LaPlante directly. "There are some who would say that you should receive the same sentence that you imposed on the Gustafson family—that is, death by ligature or hanging." For a moment, LaPlante mimicked the judge's facial expression, and some heard him chuckle under his breath. Barton's tone grew colder. "But we have no death penalty in Massachusetts. Accordingly, the sentence to be imposed is one where you spend the rest of your life behind bars with no parole, no commutations, no furloughs—that is, three consecutive life sentences."

Having heard the verdict and the sentence, Andy Gustafson slipped out of the courthouse before the judge discharged the jury, not wanting to stay any longer than necessary. At his request, two state troopers who shielded him from reporters accompanied him. It would be two years before he would grant an interview.

Judge Barton thanked the jury, noting the sacrifices the families had made in service to the Commonwealth.

On the courthouse steps, the media jumped to interview whomever they could. They yelled questions at Cilla's sisters, Christine and Beth. "Was justice done?" Christine, her eyes red, her voice hoarse from crying, blurted into the microphone thrust in her face, "It is not going to bring back Cilla and the kids."

Beth hissed her anger, "There can be no justice. The only justice would have been if it had never happened. There were four people that were killed." She did not want the public to forget that Priscilla was three months pregnant that December day.[10]

Speculation began almost immediately about a potential appeal. Actually, appeal in first-degree murder is automatic in the state of Massachusetts. The **Boston Globe** interviewed criminal lawyers, asking whether they thought LaPlante's defense was adequate and appropriate, given that his lawyers made neither an opening nor closing argument, nor presented any of their own witnesses. Most experts agreed there would be no reasonable appeal based on the quality of his legal defense during the trial.

Years later, Andy made a similar comment. "I was lucky because I didn't have to worry about a defense attorney pulling stuff that would have gotten a mistrial or won an acquittal. There's a right way to do it and a wrong way, and Sheketoff did it the right way. He didn't victimize the victims."

LaPlante's family disagreed, continuing to assert that their son was innocent. There would indeed be a full appeal five years later, and much subsequent litigation with LaPlante primarily providing his own legal defense. But with the close of the trial, the media focus diminished markedly.

A New Beginning

The end of the trial marked a turning point for Andy and Carole. They set the wedding date, one that symbolized new life, January first. They were committed to celebrating the wholeness of who they were—their previous loves, the extended families, their friends and church, finding ways to honor all these relationships.

That fall, conversations mixed excitement for the future with shadows of the past. Nighttime wailing occurred several times a week, but Andy recognized God's constant presence, the God who was in and with, through and beyond him. He contemplated the dichotomies of his life—grief and grace, destruction and reconstruction, evil and compassion.

He was less likely to attend the support group these days—not that he wasn't appreciative, but his energy was turning. Gradually his self-perception shifted. At one of his last support group meetings, he thanked the group and celebrated the changes in his life. "I am going to remarry, marry this wonderful woman who has been listening to me all these months, who has shown me such compassion and acceptance. I used to see myself as the primary victim of LaPlante's actions, but now I can separate what happened to them and what happened to me. Even though I will never forget, I will not let myself be defined by these evil acts. Carole is there for me in that journey, not replacing Cilla in any way, but she gives me hope for a future life."

The couple invited the congregation and their neighbors to the wedding ceremony and a reception in the church's fellowship hall. Closer friends and family would continue to the hotel in Gardner, the one that Andy co-owned, for dinner and an overnight party. Preparing for the wedding motivated Andy to finish refurbishing the property, which eased tensions with his business partner.

This was a season of first anniversaries of important event occurring since the murders: Billy's birthday in November, Thanksgiving, the murders themselves, Abby's birthday. More than once, Andy flew to the Vineyard to be at Angel Cottage. At Thanksgiving, he and Carole joined the family, but he left the gathering for a time to walk alone. The first weekend in December, townsfolk lit holiday decorations on the gazebo and dedicated a tree in memory of Cilla and the children. Andy and Carole stood with friends, neighbors, Chief May, and several state troopers as the group held candles and sang "Silent Night" into the dark December twilight, bringing the light that overcomes darkness. Christmas Day, the couple surrounded themselves with angels, and did what they could to enjoy each other's company.

January 1, 1989, in the sanctuary where they had honored the lives of Cilla, Abby, Billy, and Greg, where they had said goodbye to their loved ones, where in the face of death they professed their faith in God, Andy and Carole's friends and family gathered to witness a new union. The red-carpeted room, filled with Christmas poinsettias and illuminated by candlelight, pointed toward the Great Mystery. Two ministers, one chosen by each partner, stood beside Andy, as all eyes turned to the rear doors. Cilla's sister led the procession. Greg's father walked Carole down the aisle, formally giving her away. Hearing "Dearly beloved," each person felt blessed. Cilla's brother William sang praise to God in his angelic voice. After prayers and promises, Carole and Andy, still wearing their original wedding bands, transferred these to their right hands and exchanged new covenantal rings, slipping them onto their left hands. They were not leaving the marriages they had, they were not losing the love that they had known, they were instead expanding their hearts, including past and present, as they moved into the future. For those with eyes to see and ears to hear, this was an Easter celebration—proclaiming that love never dies, that new life can emerge from the tomb, that suffering and death do not have the final word, that hope and joy are real. For Carole and Andy, this was Easter in all its glory.

Andy and Carole Gustafson's wedding day,
January 1, 1989

The reception in the fellowship hall, with small sandwiches, cookies, and a cake, given by church folks as a gift to the couple, echoed Cilla and Andy's union, complete with Carole's covering Andy's face with frosting just as Cilla had done. Family and their closest friends continued on to the reception at the Gardner hotel, which now included the Abigail Dining Room, the William Conference Room, and the 'Cilla Ballroom, as well as angel carvings integrated into the decor. The wedding banquet for all generations had toasts, a grand buffet, and a large dessert table. Adults lingered into the night over drinks while the youth adjourned to their hotel rooms and ran up a tab on room service.

Soon after the wedding, Andy reached out to his sister-in-law, Christine. Christine's life had also been blown asunder by her sister's murder, both her relationships and her work life destabilized. Andy bought her a present, a carved angel. He tucked a $50 bill into the card which began, "I am so proud of you...." It was a gift she carried in her heart for years.

The yellow colonial on the green, down the street from the church, became Andy and Carole's home. They listed the Saunders Road house for sale and consolidated their belongings, filling the attic, the basement, and the garage since both of them found it hard to let go of cherished possessions from their previous lives. Some boxes stayed packed away, unopened for decades, but knowing they were there provided constancy they both needed. They took steps to transform the colonial into their shared home. They added furniture from Saunders Road and gave other pieces away. Larry, Andy, and some friends built a shed. They hired a contractor to redo the living room, adding a new semi-circular window and improving insulation.

New patterns of life evolved outside the house as well. The role of church moderator demanded additional attention as conflict arose around Neal Lund's ministry. Andy arranged help from a consultant skilled in conflict, attended listening sessions, and facilitated governing board meetings. Ultimately, the Rev. Lund resigned and a trained interim became the pastor. This turmoil seemed to churn up hurt, fear, uncertainty, and anxiety that echoed the past as much as the present. Andy had patience and sure-footedness when other people seemed emotionally reactive. Having found God's Presence in the midst of his own grief and inner conflict, he drew on his own experience, reassuring the congregation of the Holy Spirit's availability even when things seem hopeless. He spoke with an authority grounded in his own life, and people knew that. Step by step, Andy became the spiritual leader of Townsend Congregational Church.

His law practice changed, too. He decided to decline further work with his business partner and move toward dissolving that relationship. His prayers were filled with questions.

What might I do instead? What if I could use my training to protect children in need of services, to provide that care in a timely fashion? What if I could prevent other young people from ending up like Daniel LaPlante, wounded beyond repair, acting out, and hurting people? He resolved to offer his services to the Juvenile Court in Ayer, first as a guardian *ad litem* and ultimately in a range of protective services. The pay was meager, but the payoff was huge.

Andy in his mid-thirties, and Carole in her early forties, felt the biological clock ticking. They both desired children, a dream that had eluded Carole, a reality that the murders had destroyed for Andy. This future family would never replace his previous one, but it might fill his heart now.

One night, Andy wondered aloud with Carole whether he was really a good-enough father. He was thinking about an incident for which he still felt guilty.

"It was on one of our camping trips to the Cape, at Nickerson State Park," he began. "We had such fun there. It had a great bike trail. I put three-year-old Abby in the child seat of a rented bike. I admit, I was acting like a kid. I was horsing around, forgetting the risk to my daughter. Abby fell off. I felt the shift, heard the thump.

She screamed. I stopped and ran to rescue her, carrying her back to the campsite. Abby's crying calmed to a whimper. But Cilla ran to meet us, grabbing Abby from my arms, yelling at me in front of the family, almost beside herself in defense of her child. Cilla cleaned up the scrape on Abby's leg and she quickly ran off to play with her cousins. We made up that night, but Abby never rode on my bike again. Does that make me a bad father?"

Carole smirked. "You are a bad driver. It doesn't seem to matter whether you are in a car, a plane, or on a bike. But that doesn't make you a bad father. I think you were a wonderful dad, that you will be a wonderful father. I want you to be the father of my children."

After months of trying, medical tests, and hours of conversation, Andy and Carole understood that it would be unlikely that she would become pregnant by natural means. They talked about whether they could accept a child from another mother. Of course, they agreed. They decided to explore different options for adoption.

Through the traumatic year following the murder, Andy had avoided the media, having spoken publicly only at the funeral and during his court testimony, despite repeated requests. "Let the world know what has happened to you since the unthinkable events," pleaded reporters. In May of 1990, Andy relented and allowed Dana Kennedy of the Associated Press to meet with Carole and him, sharing what had happened in the two-and-a half years since the murders. The story appeared in newspapers across the country, from the *Boston Globe* to the *Los Angeles Times*. Theirs was a powerful story to tell and, by choosing to share it with the world, Andy took another step in healing.

During the interview, Andy celebrated his marriage to Carole. "I don't know whether I would have made it or not, without her.

Now I have a reason to get up in the morning, something to live for," he said to the reporter, his eyes lingering on Carole, his face soft and smiling. The reporter questioned the quickness of their marriage. Andy responded by citing how his life circumstances shaped his values. "Your life is about your relationships. When you lose them, you lose your life; in a way you either get stuck or you go on and make a new life."

Carole continued, "There were a few people in this town that were just aghast, but when you've gone through this kind of loss, you're just glad the sun is shining every day. Life becomes more precious to you. We didn't want to waste it. This is not erasing either of our pasts," as first she and then Andy pointed out the wedding rings from the previous marriages, and the ones from their shared union.

The article retold the basics of the tragedy and the rudiments of Andy's recovery. "It's a roller coaster with no highs, just different depths. It's a struggle just to get through each day."

Carole acknowledged that even though there was much new life, Andy still had bad days, even now, more than two years after the murders. "My heart grieves for him." Carole's eyes dropped and she sighed. "All I can do is hold him and tell him I love him."

The interview ended with their shared dream and hopes to have a family together.

In Search of New Family

Andy and Carole talked endlessly about adoption, seeking out people they knew who had adopted children of different ages from different locations. They called agencies, visited the library, attended adoption workshops, and asked probing questions of adoptive parents. They learned about international adoption and believed they could make that work. They discussed the challenges of adopting children in protective services, with Andy drawing on his experiences with the courts. They explored a new form of adoption that fostered relationships between adoptive and birth families, called open adoption. Wouldn't that be a great fit for us? they thought. Open adoption commits to keeping relationships among extended family alive to let love grow and expand. We are living that with the families of our previous marriages. It would seem like a natural extension for us, not uncomfortable at all, they would explain to family and friends. Yes, we know there are some in the adoption community who are uncomfortable with this arrangement, fearing ambivalent bonding, but, given that it is unlikely that we would be chosen for a typical closed adoption of a young child, this seems like a great possibility for us. They joined the Open Door Society.

Families seeking open adoption create a "Dear Birth Mother Letter" addressed to the potential adoptive mother, telling about themselves and their lives. This paints a picture of the parents, the extended family, the house, and the community, through photos, narratives, and a touch of creativity. It is a booklet that includes the potential adoptive parents' backgrounds, their hopes for the future, their personal resources, and the values offered to the child in question. In 1990, without the availability of the Internet, the family seeking an adoption would make many copies of this letter to distribute––to adoption agencies, to friends who might know friends seeking adoption, to distant pastors and relatives who might have connections. "Dear Birth Mother" letters are like seeds thrown on the winds of hope.

Andy and Carole reproduced multiple copies of their letter/ booklet, mailing some to friends and relatives, encouraging them to scatter them widely among people they knew. This letter process had already begun when they enrolled with an agency in Worcester, Lutheran Social Services, choosing it because it did not rule out this unorthodox approach and were willing to help with the prerequisite steps. Specifically, the agency was equipped to do what is called "the home study." The home study takes about four months and multiple meetings with the social worker. It meant that Andy had to talk about his history, including going back through both happy times and the violent homicide of his family. It meant that Carole had to relive her loss of Greg. The home study required them to disclose their financial challenges, submit results of their medical check-ups, and pay a home inspector to examine and report on the house. The social worker interviewed friends, family, the local church members, and business colleagues. Both Andy and Carole needed to have criminal background checks. This was a grueling project, but the end goal of readying the soil for an adoptive family made it all worthwhile.

Lutheran Social Services had good international connections as well as domestic conduits for adoptions. Andy and Carole, keeping their options open, started to investigate the processes required by China, Russia, and Guatemala, while their "Dear Birth

Mother" letter circulated in their extended network.

Friends checked in often with Carole, asking for any news, so receiving a call from one of her best friends was quite ordinary. However, the content of one particular call was unexpected. "I don't want to get your hopes up, but . . . . ." the friend began, "but, I was talking to my sister-in-law. I think you know, they adopted a child and she was particularly eager to support you. So, she has this friend who works at the Department of Justice. And one of her friend's colleagues—he's a grandfather, a grandfather of two little girls for whom he has physical custody. In fact, I think he and his wife are guardians of their daughter's children, I think that is what she said. He has been musing about putting the little girls up for adoption as a way to provide them more stability. The grand-father has heard about open adoption and thought that would fit their needs. Anyway, my sister-in-law's friend handed them your 'Dear Birth Mother' material earlier this week."

Carole's heart leaped into her throat. She had to intentionally calm down. "This is still a long shot," she reminded herself. Never-theless, she phoned Andy to share this glimmer of hope.

Days passed, no call. Hope began to wither.

One day in March, a little more than a year after their mar-riage, a few weeks after the hope-filled conversation with her good friend, Carole stayed home from work because the septic repair team had scheduled maintenance on the pipes. When the phone rang, Carole answered, expecting it to be the septic company.

"Hello," began an unfamiliar voice. "Hello. Is this Carole? Car-ole Gustafson?" The caller stumbled over the name.

"Yes. Are you coming to fix my pipes in Townsend?"

"No, no," he stammered and then took a big breath. "My name is Bernie. My wife and I received your 'Dear Birth Mother' mate-rials and we would like to talk to you and Andy."

Carole let out a little squeal, her heart racing, her voice trem-bling, her mind trying to regain composure. "Oh, that would be wonderful. What would you like to know?"

"Well, first, we wondered if you are open to taking two children?"

Carole gulped, a smile spread over her face, her will power doing whatever she could to hold in her desire to jump up and down. "Yes," Carole answered. "Yes! Definitely!"

"So, let me tell you a bit about us. As I said, I am Bernie. I live with my wife and my two younger sons in Maryland. My daughter had two daughters who, for a set of complicated reasons, now live with us. We have had guardianship of them for a while, in hopes that our daughter would get her feet under her enough to really parent them effectively. We've wrestled with our sadness and our disappointment in our daughter, but we have been charged with the well-being of these two little girls now. After much conversation and inner struggle, we have come to believe these girls will have a better life if they are adopted into a stable home. We love them very much and are particularly looking for an arrangement where our relationship could continue and perhaps, in the future, the girls could get to know their birth mother, maybe even have a relationship with her."

Carole assured Bernie that she and Andy would indeed welcome this extended set of relationships. "We have attended some open adoption workshops and have learned from families who are making this communication work." Carole referred to her family's history, citing the two rings, the pictures of both former spouses on display in the house, the extent and regularity of connections with both sets of extended families. "We define family in a very open manner," Carole concluded.

Bernie continued describing himself and his family. "I am a retired colonel. I served twenty years and now I work as a civilian. I see from your booklet that you have known military life. It looks like you once lived not far from here."

The conversation was relaxed, comfortable, and easy. They

talked for an hour, finding common background in Catholicism, in military life, in shared values around reading, even in favorite sports activities. When the phone call concluded, they agreed to talk again.

Carole screamed for joy as she got off the phone and jumped around the kitchen. Finally, she calmed enough to call Andy. Still almost too excited to speak, she blurted out, "Andy, Andy!"

"Is everything all right?" Andy asked anxiously.

"You can't believe what just happened," she said breathlessly, the words tumbling out so fast they were hard to understand. "The grandfather that my friend talked about, remember? He called me. We had the most wonderful conversation. And get this. They have two daughters that they want a home for. Two!" Andy had her repeat parts of the message so he understood.

Carole had tears in her eyes. On the other end, Andy cried, too. He came home early from the office. He picked Carol up, squeezed her, and twirled her around. Then, regaining his composure and logic, "I suppose we shouldn't get too excited. It's only one phone call."

But there were more phone calls, ones in which Andy talked to Bernie and to his wife, Joy. Each pairing conversed easily, while the strongest connection remained between Carole and Bernie.

After a week or two, Bernie and Joy decided to drive to Massachusetts for a weekend visit. The couples planned the details of their meeting, deciding that Leominster had comfortable hotels, and restaurants where they could linger. The two couples would meet face to face for breakfast at Bickford's. In the intervening days, it was hard for Andy and Carole to focus effectively on anything. They were quiet on the drive to Leominster Saturday morning, filled with hope and riddled with the dread of disappointment. The couples recognized each other immediately, and the telephone conversations translated easily into camaraderie and growing trust. They genuinely liked each other. During that meeting,

Bernie and Joy described the children, now almost four and fifteen months. They revealed more about their daughter, the events that led to the decision to seek an adoptive family, and the complicated emotions other family members had about this adoption. After breakfast, Andy drove both couples to Townsend, showing them the community, the schools, their house, the church. Sitting in the Gustafsons' living room hours after they had first met, Joy looked directly into Carole's eyes and asked a question she had hinted at in many different ways before. "How do you feel, Carole, about not adopting a baby?"

Carole was quick to answer, "I think of a fifteen-month-old as a baby."

They drove together back to Leominster. As they were leaving, Joy handed Carole pictures of the two little girls. Carole, stunned, showed them to Andy, squeezing his hand. "Oh my God, they are so beautiful." Then she thought to herself, Laura looks like a pixie and Holly, with blond curly hair, like a little angel.

"Thank you," she hugged Joy. "Thank you both."

"We'll talk soon," Joy replied as they waved goodbye. At home, Andy and Carole held each other, both crying and laughing, almost beside themselves with joy.

Do Dreams Come True?

The two households now talked regularly. Although Bernie connected to Carole and leaned toward the open adoption in Massachusetts, another potential adoptive family, a military couple who had previously met the family in Maryland, also had regular telephone contact. In the final stages of their home study, that other couple believed Bernie and Joy would choose them as the adoptive parents. It surprised them to learn of a second couple with whom they were competing.

When Carole and Andy realized that they were not the only family under consideration, they too got nervous. They remembered the workshops that stressed the tenuousness of this stage of the journey. They knew that many first contacts do not lead to adoptions, even when those contacts go well. They reminded each other to keep their excitement in check, though they knew they would be crushed if someone else parented these two little ones. They prayed together and separately, listened for guidance, asked for patience, leaned on God for strength. Carole talked with friends, sharing her feelings and taking the edge off her anxiety by seeking their advice.

When Andy met with the Rev. Dick Sparrow to prepare for the county-level meeting of the church, the conversation turned to Andy's personal life. "I relate to Job a lot these days." Andy gazed away for a few moments. "How Job gets pulled between his relationship with his friends and his relationship with God. All logic fails and there is this tangle of questions. But when Job faces into the mystery that is beyond his comprehension and lives into the paradox on God's terms, somehow pieces begin to come together in a new way. At night, I still cry and moan, missing my family. It just comes on me, even more than two years later. But there is this new world opening too, particularly when I dream that Carole and I might, just might, create this family. I feel like it could collapse, but it has been a very exciting time, a time of bonding and joy for Carole and me. And my dreams reassure me that Cilla, Abby, and Billy are angels guiding the process."

About two weeks later, Joy and Bernie invited the Gustafsons to visit them in Maryland. Andy and Carole suspected that they would be scrutinized by the extended family, a family who would be asked for their observations and opinions after the weekend was over.

Andy and Carole's conversation on the drive to Maryland swung wildly. On one hand, Carole tapped her deep longings and celebrated her connection to Bernie. In her mind's eye, she had created elaborate images of family time with these two beautiful little girls. On the other hand, she felt terrified of losing the children to the other family, of having her dreams shattered yet again. And they hadn't met the children, hadn't seen how they behaved, didn't know how they would feel about each other face to face. But, if they were too self-protective, they wouldn't be showing the family, and more importantly the little girls, the love that was already growing inside them. Somehow in the midst of this, Andy found words, something almost coming through him, "We have to walk this in faith, trusting in whatever happens, knowing that God will give us the strength we need no matter what." Vulnerability, no matter how risky, was the path. It was the perspective they both needed then.

Arriving in Maryland the night before the meeting, they stayed in a motel not far from the restaurant selected for the rendezvous. What sleep they got was fitful, with many details running through their anxious minds. How does one dress to meet one's potential new family? Andy felt more self-conscious than he did when he met Cilla's parents. On the way to the car, Carole straightened Andy's collar and Andy wiped a bit of face cream off Carole's face. They drove to the restaurant early and waited near the door. Bernie and Joy drove in, their van loaded with six people. Two tall teenage boys spilled out. Bernie carried the baby. Joy released the four year old from her car seat and held her hand as they crossed the parking lot. Carole reached for Andy's hand and squeezed it, both donning ear-to-ear smiles. Carole whispered, "They are so perfect. More adorable in person than in the pictures."

Joy introduced her sons and then said, "Laura and Holly, I want you to meet Carole and Andy Gustafson. They have driven from Massachusetts to be with us." At first, the little girls smiled shyly and hid behind their uncles, but in a matter of moments one of the boys broke the tension.

"I want pancakes for breakfast."

"Me, too. Me, too," echoed four-year-old Laura.

"I want blueberry. And hot chocolate," added the other teen.

Andy chimed in, "I'm hungry, too. I was thinking about chocolate-chip pancakes." The kids looked surprised, but Carole just giggled.

They found a big table, ordered breakfast, and began to relax. They laughed, drew pictures and played peek-a-boo. Andy and Carole answered questions about life in Townsend that the boys asked. This meeting didn't seem to faze the little girls, who did not understand the importance of what was happening.

Both families adjourned to the grandparents' house. Here, life returned to normal, with games with the uncles, toys dragged into the living room, and books read aloud. Joy's mother, Alma, joined them for lunch. Alma, in her eighties, lived around the corner and up the street. A southern lady, a hard worker, and a well-connected great-grandmother, she loved those little girls, and she more than anyone else was heart broken at the prospect of her great-granddaughters' moving hundreds of miles away. She wasn't sure anyone could parent these children the way she wanted them to be cared for, especially out of her sight. And she didn't think this open adoption process would really work. She let her doubts be known to all who would listen. Perhaps she more than the others felt loss more than gain in such an arrangement.

A few days after this visit, Bernie and Joy called Carole. "I want you to know we have made a decision." Carole held her breath. "We want you and Andy to be Laura and Holly's adoptive parents."

Tears streamed down Carole's face. "Oh, thank you. It is such an honor and a dream come true." After a bit of chatting, Carol added, "Our home study is nearly done."

Now daily phone calls included the children, especially Laura. Carole and Andy returned to Maryland to spend time with the family and to take the girls out by themselves, to a playground, to a restaurant, then home for bedtime stories and a routine that would be continued by phone from that day on.

With the home study complete and Bernie and Joy committed, Carole and Andy made one last visit to Maryland, taking the children to stay at a hotel with them. They chose one with a swimming pool, hoping to splash and giggle together. The swimming pool was closed, but they made it fun anyway. More importantly, they told the girls about the upcoming changes. They showed them pictures of their house and their dog, told them about how they would be their forever mommy and daddy, and promised that they would be coming back in two weeks to bring them to Massachusetts.

On Memorial Day weekend in May in 1990, Carole, Andy, Holly, and Laura became a family.

The new parents picked up the children in Maryland and drove directly to Martha's Vineyard, to Angel Cottage. Both Andy and Carole put work on the back burner to focus on the children, in order to create stability for them. In the protective environment of the Oak Bluff Methodist Campground, they bonded as a family. They went to the beach, walked to a playground, read stories in the living room, snuggled before bed. It was a remarkably smooth transition. Andy and Carole

Carole, Andy, Laura and Holly Gustafson, circa 1990.

kept pinching themselves, feeling so fortunate, but afraid it was going too easily, as they waited for a bomb to drop.

Andy returned to Townsend several times, doing law work, checking in with people at the church, making sure the house was O.K. By the time the family returned from the Vineyard, Andy had left his law office and moved his practice into their house. Both he and Carole would play a significant role in the care of these daughters.

During the initial adjustment period, Andy and Carole phased out the connection with the family in Maryland, to establish the new primary bond for the children. Starting with daily bedtime phone calls to the grandparents to say goodnight, mirroring the ones that Andy and Carole had made during the spring, they dropped to several times a week, to once a week. The children bonded, but Great-Grandma Alma kept calling. She had not been to Massachusetts, had not seen the house and the town, had not accepted this adoption. Bernie and Joy expressed their confidence in the care the children would receive. Andy and Carole reassured Alma that she would be able to see the children several times a year, but she kept calling almost every day. The grandparents and the new parents strategized. Perhaps if Alma could see the new home for herself she would be more comfortable, they posited. So, Joy and Alma came to Townsend to visit in late August, hoping this would provide the needed reassurance. Still, the calls continued. Finally, the new family set a limit. No calls for two weeks, then no more than once a week for the fall. The whole family could visit, once in October and then around Christmas. In time, Alma grew to accept Laura and Holly's new home, and she gained a sense of peace and even joy about her great granddaughters' family. In a few months, the Gustafsons completed the required waiting time and the documents for legal adoption. This was the light that overcame the darkness for the grandparents, Andy, Carole, and the two children.

The New Normal

A ndy and Carole, Laura and Holly established the rhythms of stable family life. Carole took primary responsibility for parenting the girls, providing structure and routine, while Andy excelled at being a calming presence. Church was central. Andy moderated council meetings, the couple pitched in at fundraisers, and Holly and Laura participated in the children's program. In June of 1991, Andy and Carole brought their daughters to be baptized. In the square sanctuary, surrounded again by the church and extended family, they celebrated the outward, visible sign of grace, the sacrament of baptism—Laura and Holly's new life as beloved children within the eternal family of God. Another resurrection moment.

Andy's work life took on new meaning and direction. He teamed with others to launch Hope Adoption in Worcester, wanting the open approach to become more accessible, visible, and straightforward than it had been in traditional agencies. He joined forces with social workers who would provide home studies, strengthened connections to the Department of Social Services, presented at adoption conferences, and shared his personal experiences freely. He focused on the legal side of open adoptions, untangling complicated paper work as well as providing emotional support in complex situations. He wanted to bring healing. He said to a reporter in retrospect, "I felt if I could get kids on the right path, they wouldn't go on the same path LaPlante went on." As open adoption gained acceptance, his adoption agency merged with others in Worcester.

Andy also applied his legal skills through the Massachusetts Committee for Public Counsel Services. He defended the rights of children in need of support, children in challenging home situations, children who were hard for parents to control, children in the custody of the Department of Social Services. He met with families, agencies, probation officers, and youth. He advocated for secure placements, psychological services, supervised visits, and effective school programs. He committed his energy to protecting the youngest and most vulnerable. His deep compassion and perspective, the fruits of his own suffering, offered a reliable presence in emotionally complex and even violent circumstances.

At home, he played with the children, read books, listened to them think and grow.

Laura had a way of getting into scrapes and Andy loved her through these rough places, always pointed out her strengths and the ways her challenges were just like what any child had to face. One time when her impulsiveness got her into trouble, Andy decided to tell her a story about himself.

Andy with Holly, circa 1993

With Laura on his lap, he began, "You know Uncle Larry, right? Did you know he is my brother, just like Holly is your sister?"

"No, is he?"

"Yes, but he is older than I am. And when we were growing up, he didn't like what I did all the time."

"I don't like what Holly does sometimes," Laura mused.

"I know. Sometimes it is hard to have sisters. And Larry would say, sometimes he didn't like me as a brother, either. So, he and my dad were doing this special thing, getting ready for the Boy Scouts to go camping. And they were bringing all the gear to the back yard to get ready."

"Like we do when we go to the Saco." Laura made a picture in her mind.

"I think I was jealous of how my older brother got all of my father's attention. And I was curious, too. So I went to investigate. I asked my father why they needed all this gear, and he told me that Scouts needed to be prepared. Prepared for any kind of weather. So, I decided to help and was just doing what my dad and the other Scouts were doing. I climbed up on the pile and started opening kits. I'd seen the older boys doing it. Why couldn't I do it, too? But the older Scouts didn't like that.

"One of them yelled at me. 'Get away from here. You are bothering us. You aren't welcome. You are too young.'"

"I wouldn't like that," Laura volunteered, her face looking serious.

"I didn't either and I started to slink away, with tears in my eyes. And then I got an idea. I knew where my mom stored the garden hose. I pulled it out, turned on the water, and sprayed the equipment."

"That was great, Dad!" Laura cheered.

"Well," Andy continued, "it did feel kind of good and it did have some logic. But you know what happened next. They had to dry all that gear out and it was hard for them. My dad had to do a whole lot more work and he wasn't happy. I learned that I needed to think about other people's feelings as well as my own when I make decisions. And you know what?"

"No, what?"

"I learned to do that better, step by step. And so can you."

Father and daughter were deeply bonded. Even as a twenty something, Laura would say, "Dad, you're my best friend."

Andy with Laura, circa 1994

Andy found lots of ways to be a child advocate. He learned the intricacies of the special-education laws. After attending a workshop in Washington, DC, he applied those laws to Individual Educational Programs (IEPs), gaining skills in mediating disputes between families and schools, always advocating for the rights of children. He attended IEP meetings as a legal advocate and as one who highlighted children's gifts more than their deficits. He provided support to children referred by the courts, as well as assisting friends and family with children who needed special services.

In the evolving new normal, friends came over to play Scrabble or cards. They attended church suppers, band concerts, town parades, and Sunday worship. At the church, Andy provided support for administrative functions and, increasingly, spiritual leadership. He sensed the need to stop for prayer. Because Andy could see the blessings of the moment, name the ways the church served in the community, proclaim the hope for the future, and remind everyone that what the church did mattered in transforming lives, people found God in the Townsend Congregational Church. Yes, many who knew Andy's first family, who had lived through those horrific events, still reverberated with that trauma, their sense of safety impaired; but then they would be reminded that if Andy could pick up the pieces, if Andy could choose to live, if Andy could be loving, grateful, and joyful, perhaps they could be too.

While family life was well grounded, their finances were more tenuous. One night, while Andy and Carole were wrestling with bills, Andy confessed a story to Carole. It was one of the more tense times that he and Cilla had had. "It was around the time that my cousin Tom joined the law practice. I thought if we expanded and added an assistant, finances would improve. Besides, I really needed the skills that Marianne brought as a paralegal. She was so organized, knowledgeable, and she added a cheerful efficiency to the practice. But it also added more cost.

"One night, behind closed doors, the tensions around money exploded. Cilla burst into tears over unpaid bills, stomping her foot in frustration. It was a tough interchange, not a usual happening between us, and I think I still feel guilt about that time. But Cilla was amazing. As she calmed down, we prayed together the way we did almost every night. When we finished, she looked at me. 'I guess I have to do something about this.' The next day, she dropped Abby off at a sitter and took a job as a clerk at the drug store. A few months later, she interviewed for and accepted the head teacher position at Townsend Cooperative Playschool. I guess there was a silver lining, because she connected again with her passion in teaching; this was a job in which she thrived. Children and parents loved her, and she found the work a blessing. But, she maintained a few hours on the weekend at the drug store. I guess I quietly felt that I had not lived up to my self-concept of being a good provider. Somehow, I want to do it differently with us."

They discussed selling two things Andy loved: his interest in the Cessna and Angel Cottage. Relinquishing the plane and any remaining claims on the hotel would sever the ties with his former business partner and net a small amount of money. The plane had been a dream as well as an asset. The cottage had deep emotional ties. These were nostalgic and value-clarifying conversations. Andy smiled as he recalled flying from Townsend to the Vineyard in those difficult days. It had been his refuge, a place where he could be himself apart from media, work, and community demands. He would miss the freedom of impulsive plane trips and the connection to Cilla and the kids that the angel gingerbread provided. And yet, he knew his highest priority was supporting his current family. He decided to let go of the plane and to list angel cottage. It didn't take long. With a mixture of sadness and relief, he transferred the lease on both and moved on to the next chapter of their lives.

Sometime in the mid-1990s, Andy attempted to write his life story, from the violent murders to his road to new life. He created a book proposal that received initial approval and started to work with an editor. Carole remembers the notes spread all over the table as he grappled with putting words to paper. He brought out picture albums and mementos, but seeing them made him cry. Writing from memory was easier, but it still triggered difficult emotions that stayed with him for days. His sister recalls discussing his efforts, hoping they would help him take another step in healing. No one seems to know what happened exactly, but everyone agrees the process stopped. One person thought his editor left that publishing house. Another wondered if the pain stymied him. A third blamed the 1993 appeal of LaPlante's life sentence, stimulating the public retelling of the murder. No one knows for sure. No one knows the whereabouts of Andy's notes. Could he have destroyed them? Carole looked for them on many different occasions, but has not found them.

Is God Calling?

Andy, Carole, Holly, Laura,
circa 1998

There was a rhythm to their life. The children went to school and Carole and Andy to work. They had friends, church, and the outdoors. Near the end of school that year, Holly's class was doing a project that would last all summer. It was based on the book *Flat Stanley* by Jeff Brown, and a literacy project started in the mid 1990s. The book tells of a boy, Stanley, who has a bulletin board land on him in the middle of the night that squashes him flat. Stanley's family has to adjust to this new reality. It turns out that being flat has its advantages. It means he can go on all sorts of adventures. In the class, the children made their own Flat Stanley and received instructions to take photos wherever they went that summer. This became Holly and Andy's project. Together, they created a cardboard figure of a boy about a foot tall, with arms and legs that moved because of paper fasteners placed at the joints, and a Red Sox baseball cap.

Summer fun, circa 1996

Flat Stanley particularly like traditional family camping trips with Uncle Larry and Aunt Shelley, Grandpa Len and Grandma Shirley nearby. They caught some great photos with people sitting around the picnic table, protected from the weather by the big pavilion tent. Flat Stanley got to cook on the grill and kayak with Dad. Flat Stanley took rides on the playground equipment and read stories in the tent. Flat Stanley went for hikes in the woods and for walks on the beach. He even went to church—a memorable summer.

Andy and Carole parented together, enjoyed each other's company, supported each other in their work, and were each other's best friend. Carole continued to give Andy room when his grief intruded into his sleep, now not that often, but occasionally nightmares and wailing fits were triggered by who knew what. Andy was grateful for Carole's patience and support. Carole was likewise grateful for Andy's patience and support, particularly of her mothering. They shared a wonderful love.

Because he was both an administrative and a spiritual leader of the church, Andy's decision to be a spokesperson for financial stewardship at Townsend surprised no one. He smiled at how God was leading him. He, who had previously been quiet about his faith, spoke to the whole congregation because the church needed that. He who struggled with personal finances modeled generosity based on his gratitude for God's grace. He who often played the class clown inspired listeners to reflect on their personal beliefs, to speak their gratitude, to recognize God's grace moving in their lives. This was true not only in Townsend, but also in his work with the regional church. He noticed how the administrative and legal tasks of the Central Association brought him meaning and joy, and how people in those circles responded to his spiritual reflections. He began to wonder whether God was pointing him, calling him toward ordained ministry in the church he loved and prized. On the other hand, he believed strongly that the ministry of church members was just as important as the work of the clergy. It depended on what God wanted. Andy believed that listening for God's will happens best when shared with others.

At a lunch with the Rev. Dick Sparrow, where they talked about both association business and personal reflections, Andy shared encounters he had had with God that shifted and guided his path. "Work has become more meaningful, and I sense being led into future possibilities." He took a long pause and then blurted out, "I think I may be called to the ministry."

Dick had learned never to be surprised at such conversations and approached them with gentle discernment, listening, asking open-ended questions, and eventually coming back to a variation of one question he considered crucial. "Do you think you want to serve a local church? I don't hear you talking about that exactly."

Andy paused. "I don't think that is it. It is something else, but I am not sure. I just am passionate about what the church has to offer people."

"Well," Dick was careful in choosing his words, "if there is something else you can do other than serve a local church that will give you as much joy, then that is what you should pursue. There are so many different ways to be in ministry in the church. Ordination is specifically for those set aside for the ministry of Word and Sacrament, most fully carried out in the local parish."

Dick's message was what he said to almost anyone who began a conversation about "call." Andy heard it more personally. He heard that ordained ministry didn't fit, but perhaps there was something else he could do with and for the church. He continued to offer his gifts to the Central Association and increasingly to the state-level conference office in Framingham.

Andy loved to kayak. circa 2000

Andy had found joy in the woods and the rivers since he was a boy. Particularly in the years following the murders, Andy found solace and peace in outdoor activities—hiking, paddling, cross-country skiing. He relished the family camping trips with their ready access to floats and canoes, but the kayak was Andy's personal favorite. The flow of the river, the nearness of nature, the rhythm of his body moving his boat through the water brought serenity. Some years, he entered kayak races, especially the local one sponsored by the Lion's Club. A master kayaker, he won or placed in that race several times. Paddling the Westfield Whitewater Race with his brother, he officially earned the title of River Rat. Wherever he went, a hat covered his bald head. He had a whole wardrobe of hats. Outdoors, Andy, let go of his burdens and responsibilities, let go of attending to the needs of others, let go of his to do list and his anxieties. Let go. Sabbath.

Near the end of the 1990s, the Townsend Congregational Church went through another transition, with one minister leaving, a time of interim and search, and the selection of the Rev. Gail Kendrick as the new settled pastor. Gail tended to the personal needs in the congregation, and her quiet presence reduced anxiety. The church, now more unified, looked toward the future. Andy shared his vision for the church with her. What if they refurbished the building: put in an elevator, built more rooms for a nursery school, created a fellowship hall that could be used by the whole town? He painted a picture of the church reaching out to its neighbors: serving inexpensive monthly suppers, reopening a preschool, offering programs for retired community members. This vision required an ambitious capital campaign. Could they do that? Some voiced doubts, but Andy inspired confidence, enthusiasm, and generosity in the church, and in the town.

Some church leaders envisioned something bigger than re-furbishing the building. Andy became the spokesperson. "Our faith," he asserted, "is not just about changing our lives, it's about changing the lives of people outside our circle. I have shared my practice of tithing my personal income to God's work through the church. Likewise, I believe that God would have us tithe our cap-ital building campaign as well. I support the Outreach Commit-tee's proposal to include $50,000 of the $500,000 goal for causes beyond ourselves. I've heard many in the congregation dreaming of sponsoring a Habitat for Humanity house. I believe tithing our campaign will fulfill this dream."

Andy's energy and vision aligned with those of others in the congregation, and multiplied. The proposal was simultaneously exciting and scary. Could a little church promise to fund a Hab-itat house by itself? I don't think so, some muttered. But others thought, if Andy can do what he's done, we can do great things, too. The church agreed to those goals.

Andy and Carole were not only generous givers, they were also willing to ask others. Andy in particular had no difficulty looking into the eyes of friends, sharing with them how essential the church had been in his life, how important it was to the fu-ture, how, together, Christ's followers carry the light, the light that overcomes darkness. Andy's palpable faith got others to consider their choices more deeply, to notice the hold fear had on them, to claim their priorities, to risk thinking in new ways, stretching their capacity for generosity.

A church couple, Melanie and Don, took leadership with the Habitat House. They didn't do it in the way Habitat folks thought would work. They had not collected the amount of money Habitat projected would be needed to fund building a new house. Instead, builders and companies promised services and materials pro bono. Habitat considered donations in kind unreliable. That warn-ing raised doubts in the congregation. "Would there be enough?"

Andy focused on abundance and not scarcity, and his faith was contagious. With creativity, persistence, and good humor, the leadership recruited additional local workers and trades people, and secured additional donations from small businesses outside of the town. The excavating equipment, the forms and footings for the foundations, as well as truckloads of concrete appeared on schedule. Work crews from the church, volunteers from town, teens from youth groups, the promised skilled workers, and the family selected to receive the house contributed to the effort. The joyful spirit of a community-supported project radiated out into the homes of volunteers, the businesses who provided services, the coffee shops where stories were swapped, the grocery store where photos of the project appeared on the community bulletin board.

Between the in-kind donations and the $25,000 raised by the capital campaign, the Townsend Congregational Church funded a whole Habitat house for a local refugee family from Eastern Europe. They got to know the family and learned the family's story. They hired the mom to provide childcare in their Sunday School. Building this Habitat house changed lives for the better—not just the lives of a family with a difficult history who became homeowners, but also those of the people who worked together to create the house. And all it took was generosity, the generosity of time, talent, and treasure. Andy had told them this in the abstract, but now they had experienced the joy.

Although there were many missions that Andy and Carole supported, it was the Relay for Life that was closest to Carole's heart. It was her way to honor Greg. This nation-wide event sponsored by the American Cancer Society gathers teams of walkers and runners to honor survivors of cancer, to remember those who have lost their lives to this disease, and to raise money for research. The springtime contest takes a year of planning that culminates in a twenty-four-hour relay race during which one person from each team stays on the track around the clock in recognition that cancer never sleeps. For years, Carole and Andy carted their pop-up trailer to the race so the children could sleep while they took turns walking the track. Over time, Laura and Holly got involved, first walking one loop in the daytime, then assisting with the fundraising and eventually, becoming more active team members. Family and friends launched silly, creative or outrageous fundraisers that would engage the community—such as flocks of plastic pink flamingos or decorated toilets on people's lawns, harnessing playful energy to fight cancer.

A Dream Job

The children grew. Andy encouraged Holly's horseback riding and danced with her at a father-daughter event. He applauded at Laura's track and gymnastics meets. He worked beside them on homework and on mission projects at church. All through those years, Andy and Carole modeled the practices of open adoption, first staying connected to the children's extended family and ultimately reuniting the girls with their birth mother. The grandparents and uncles came to Massachusetts several times a year, including a visit around Christmas. Carole, Andy, and the girls traveled to Maryland regularly. Sometime in the mid 1990s, the girls' biological mother began to heal, to move ahead, and to ask questions about her daughters. Grandparents Bernie and Joy suggested that Holly and Laura meet their mother, and Carole and Andy agreed. During a Maryland visit, the biological mother and daughters reconnected. Laura remembered her mother and eagerly sat next to her as they read stories together. Holly clung to Carole or Andy. The three adults and two children stayed together for the first visits. Gradually, Laura and Holly spent time alone with their biological mother, enjoying short times in the park, ice cream cones and eventually staying over night at her home. As the new millennium approached, the birth mother grew strong, married, and had another child. Exchange visits continued in various constellations both in Maryland and Massachusetts. As the relationship strengthened, Laura, now a young teen, requested a longer visit with her mother in Maryland. This arrangement became a regular summer experience, with Laura and Holly going together and separately. For all involved, open adoption broadened their sense of family, of belonging, of finding love in the world.

During Andy's fifteen years of involvement with the regional and state-level church, he got to know many of the paid staff. He particularly appreciated the ministry of Steven Gray, who provided leadership for Stewardship and Finance for the conference. Gray assisted Townsend with its capital campaign and led stewardship workshops that Andy found helpful. When Andy heard that Steven was leaving his post and that the conference was accepting applications for the position of associate conference minister for Stewardship and Finance, Andy was intrigued. He studied the job description, thought of his passion for stewardship, recognized that his legal background would be an asset, and reflected on the value he placed on proclaiming God's grace. Perhaps he could serve the church he loved with joy in this position without ordination, the way that Dick Sparrow had suggested. As he envisioned working with the state-level staff in Framingham, supporting local churches, telling stories about the ministries of the wider church, and sharing the joy it brought to be part of the Body of Christ, his excitement grew; but almost simultaneously, his doubts grew as well. It wasn't the needs of his family that interfered with his plans. His daughters were teens and doing fine. Instead, he doubted himself, his gifts, his perspective, his personality. Would he be a good fit for the task? Could he live up to the expectations for a conference minister? Did he have the people skills needed to interact with so many individuals, and the theological grounding needed in that role? His training differed from those with a Masters of

Divinity.

Andy set up an appointment with Pastor Gail to get her point of view. They chatted for a while about the next council agenda, about prayer concerns, about his family. Then he brought up the real reason he was there.

"I read the job description for Associate Conference Minister for Stewardship and Finance, and...." He bit his lip a bit. "Do you think I could do that job? Do I have the gifts?"

He paused, looked down, fiddled with his fingers, preparing himself for a negative reply.

"Of course you do. You'd be amazing. I think of all you have offered this congregation."

"Really?" He looked up and smiled. The pace of his speech increased. "Oh, terrific. I think it's my dream job. I think it's where I am called. Would you write a recommendation?"

"Of course, I would be honored," Gail answered, while simultaneously becoming aware of her own ambivalence. Andy's focus on the larger church would mean he would not have as much energy for Townsend, and she had grown to rely on him.

Andy applied for the job. His first interview went well. He made a great impression with his lovely smile and the directness and sincerity of his presentation. The committee narrowed the pool and requested a demonstration for the second interview. "Show us how you would link people's spirituality to stewardship efforts." This challenge fired up Andy's creative juices, and he concocted a game. Carole remembers the multiple hours he put into preparing Stump the Steward. He presented the game to a powerhouse interview team. "Choose a Bible passage, any passage, and I will make the connections," Andy challenged, and the group rose to the occasion. There were passages from Judges and Job, from Psalms and Song of Solomon. As if he were playing tennis, Andy would hit the volleys back, some with a lob, and some with a smash.

Andy showed himself to be so grounded in the Bible, so alive with his faith, so present to each person in the room, so filled with joy that an unspoken unity arose when the interview was complete. When Andy left the room, the committee members looked at each other. "There's our guy." No debate, no comparison, just amazement at what God had brought.

Despite the thorough background checks, most of the interview committee did not know Andy's tragic story at that time. They knew only that he was a lawyer who had worked in protective services. It wasn't until later that his personal history and the work in the conference would be linked. Even though some people had heard rumors, few could have guessed his back-story, given the quick wit, the easy smile, the generosity of shared leadership. He would only tell that story later, and then mostly as a foundation of other reflections, built on the assumption that people already knew the details of his history.

Andy spoke at many churches in Massachusetts

Andy's work as a conference minister had a multitude of facets and kept evolving over the ten years he held the position. He was a learner, open to what God was doing in the world—with technology, with ecumenical partnerships, with changing needs, with the evolving role of the conference. Much of the time he worked with local congregations, providing support for programs relating to stewardship and generosity. There were weeks when he visited more than a half-dozen churches, typically meeting with local stewardship committees or mission teams to foster generous giving. He might review and add to programs already in place; he might help a congregation consider the various types of stewardship drives that other congregations found successful; he might give examples of narrative budgets; he might talk about how the mission work of the state, national, and local church changes lives.

As much time as Andy spent on the road visiting churches, he worked many hours at the Framingham Conference Center. Typically, he kept the door to his office open and could be heard, many doors away, moving his chair around, talking to himself, singing in his off-key way. He welcomed people who dropped by, often coming out of his office to greet them. He listened to visitors and staff alike. His energy and presence made him different from most of the colleagues who had graced those halls in recent years. A student visiting from a Boston Theological polity class, Victoria Gaisford, remembered her visit vividly. "It was the first time I met Andy, and he made such an impression on me. He was genuine, fully attentive, and present. And his laugh! Everyone responded to his laugh—students, teachers and the staff there. He was so easy-going. He stood out as different from the other staff we met."

Andy and Peter Wells, the area minister from the western part of the state, formed a fast friendship. Although Peter's work centered elsewhere, he came to Framingham once or twice a week. When he arrived, he and Andy were drawn together like magnets. They would visit people's offices, walk or even prance up and down the hallways filling the whole place with loud chatter and laughter. He and Peter bounced off each other with humor, creative ideas, and physical energy. The voltage went up when both of them were in the office.

These two shared their whole selves with each other—work, family, recreation, spiritual life. Often, Andy talked through difficulties and then flipped the situation to bring a laugh. He typically brought lunch from home, grabbing some leftovers or a frozen low calorie dinner. That meal could be heating in the microwave when Peter showed up. Andy would put that lunch back in the refrigerator and off they'd go to the Asian restaurant near by. Andy would pile his plate high and before you knew it, the food had disappeared, almost vacuumed off his plate. That always amazed Peter.

As accepted as he felt among the conference staff, Andy recognized that he worked among ordained ministers and that he didn't have their training. His way of turning any difficult feeling such as this awkwardness into humor showed up at a multi-state staff retreat. As Andy strolled with other staff before the morning meeting, he quipped to one of the Connecticut Conference leaders, "I'm not sure I really want to be walking with all you minister types. I don't want to get raptured by mistake."

But even with all that playfulness, Andy accomplished a lot. He planned training for lay people and clergy, and coordinated work at the national, state, county, and local levels. He joined a network of churches from many denominations to create ecumenical stewardship events.

The Conference Minister of Stewardship and Finance

A new church started on the urban streets of Worcester, serving the marginally housed and linking people in indoor churches with those who worshipped outdoors. The founding pastor, Liz Magill, spun out her dream with Andy listening, asking clarifying questions, celebrating how her vision embodied the Kingdom. He suggested ways to support the ministry financially, and shared a list of people with whom Liz might speak. After almost an hour, Liz decided to pop the question, which had been her ulterior motive for seeking out Andy, a request she expected him to decline because of his busy schedule. "Would you be willing to be on our board?" she asked tentatively.

"How could I say no to you, Liz?" he replied.

Andy became a faithful and resourceful member of the board of Worcester Fellowship, spreading the Good News on the streets of Worcester.

Andy discovered his great passion for programs of the church that impacted hurting people. He had received so much support from his own church, he knew it was life saving. The forms of this varied widely, but it gave his life meaning to be part of the larger work of God in the world. When Hurricane Katrina hit the Gulf Coast and 80% of the city was affected, Andy responded to the need directly. I was blessed to accompany him and Shantia

Wright-Gray to New Orleans in 2005 to set up a mission partnership with Good Shepherd UCC in Metairie, Louisiana.

The three of us slept in the church, each finding our own small room, two on couches and the other on a blow-up mattress. We showered in the newly installed unit built to support future mission teams, and used the toiletries in the Church World Services health kit, conveniently placed by the stall. We worshipped in the gym, with much wallboard removed in a mold-remediation project following the flooding. Worshippers sat in rows of metal folding chairs, the basketball hoops pulled toward the ceiling, the microphones amplifying the musicians and the speakers, and prayer quilts sent by churches from around the United States hanging on the walls in solidarity. Shantia brought greetings and encouragement from Massachusetts, telling the congregation of our dream for a mission partnership and thanking them for their hospitality.

After worship, a large group of lay people discussed the five-year mission proposal. Then, four leaders took us to a local restaurant, wanting us to experience the culinary prowess for which New Orleans is known. Had we tried jambalaya, crawfish étouffée, fried oysters or po' boys? Andy was delighted. We ordered an array of these favorites. Waiting for our food, we caught a glimpse of a display of t-shirts. Could we bring home a t-shirt design to build energy? What slogan would carry our message? We brainstormed, and stumbled onto "Hurricane Recovery is a Marathon, not a Sprint." Andy beamed. We had a mission campaign.

In 2005, there was a turnover in the leadership of the Massachusetts Conference. When Andy learned that the new minister and president, Jim Antal, was a vegetarian, he quipped, "Great. More meat for me." Andy won the respect of Jim quickly, but Jim found managing Andy and his colleague Peter Wells together more complicated. It was both a delight and a challenge to have the pair together. They wandered the halls, stopping to chat with staff, yukking it up with anyone who would join them. This was never subtle or quiet. Even behind closed doors, anyone could hear the antics. It brought life, creativity, and more than a little unpredictability. For example, once, on a staff-retreat day, the group entered a time of centering prayer while walking the labyrinth. Another minister moved slowly and prayerfully through the winding path to the center. Andy and Peter, on the other hand, bounded across the lines, delighted they had gotten to the middle. They had walked the labyrinth their own way, but it definitely disrupted the intended mood. There seemed no way to "control" them.

Under Jim Antal's leadership, one person often took the role of theologian at staff meetings. Andy volunteered for this often and was quite adept, adding a rich depth to the group's reflection. After the Virginia Tech shootings in 2007, the staff bemoaned the lack of gun control, and discussed ways the church could take a stand on the issue. When Andy offered his theological reflection, he began with a moment of silence, and then asked questions that were different from those the group had been considering.

"I wonder," he began, "what was missing in the shooter's life. Did he receive love and safety as he grew up? Did he have access to the mental health services he needed?" Those questions changed the perspective within the circle, like a flashlight peering through a dark room. Another staff member led prayer, opening hearts to all people involved—including the shooter—asking God for healing of individuals, families, the school, and the country.

Andy's role as associate conference minister included preaching in local churches. Usually, Andy told stories of people who inspired generosity, reported on mission work that changed lives, reminded people of the importance of the local church, and grounded all he said in the Gospel, regularly proclaiming the Good News. His open heart and his authenticity carried power.

He found he could inspire people in western Massachusetts and metro Boston as much as he could in his home church. His confidence grew, while he remained the most humble of souls.

A few years after he began his conference work, Andy risked referring to his personal tragedy within some sermons. Typically, his sermon began with the stories of generosity and examples of mission. Then, sometimes, he would tell the barest details of his life story. It might have sounded like this.

"I don't know how many of you know, but about twenty years ago, my wife and two children were murdered in our home, killed by a teen who lived less than a half a mile away. It was the church that got me through that tragedy. The caring of church people and the faith I had learned over the years let me find the God who was present, crying with me. Where can I go from Thy Presence? If I go to the farthest reaches of the sea, God will be there, prays the Psalmist. I learned that God's light shines in the darkness and evil cannot overcome it, that there is a love stronger than death.

"This shared ministry we have, our ministry locally, our ministry nationally and globally, is important, and supporting it is crucial because it touches our neighbors, heals the hurting, transforms lives. That is the reason for us to be generous with our time, talent, and treasure. It makes a difference in this world, a big difference. It made a difference in my life and many other lives."

The year 2007 marked the twentieth anniversary of the murders. Andy granted an interview to Jack Minch, a reporter for the local paper, the *Sentinel and Enterprise*. Most of the article summarized the events of 1987 that had been previously published, including a few graphic details and descriptions. Andy, on the other hand, used the interview to witness publicly to God's love alive in his life. He spoke reflectively about the Townsend Congregational Church's practical involvement in his healing, and about his relationship with the Holy, built on the strong practices he had developed as Cilla's husband. "That gave me the foundation to survive losing her," Andy said in the interview. "That was her legacy, I think."

He shared his conviction that life after death was real and his faith that he and his family would reunite some day. But Andy admitted that grief with its accompanying guilt and rage had never left him. He had, however, learned to cope. He had not lost his ability to function. "(LaPlante) could take them, but he couldn't stop my hope, life, faith, and building a new life," Andy asserted.

"Do you think about meeting LaPlante face to face? What about forgiving him?" asked the reporter.

"As far as I've come, I don't think I've come far enough to deal with that," he said. "I've still got more miles to go in my journey."

Each time Andy revisited the story publicly, he took another step in healing. It was less clear whether the retelling helped those around him. The grief buried in the town, in those who were close to the family before 1987, in those whose sense of safety had been smashed—for those people, Andy's reflection resurfaced raw emotions, unresolved fears, all those difficult memories from twenty years before. This was particularly evident in the online comments responding to the article, many of which voiced anger at the reporter for retelling this story and stirring up the terror and grief from those events. Yes, there were some gruesome details in the news article and one could ask whether it was more sensationalized than it needed to be, but it was also a story of Andy's ability to keep living, and to do so with joy.

Seven years later, as I researched this book, I found similar dynamics. For some people close to these events, it seemed irreverent to bring those memories to mind, to touch again the deep feelings of helplessness, loss and terror, as well as the destruction of the sense of safety. It was just too painful. It is as if many in the town coped by covering up this part of themselves. Andy made a different choice. He felt the emotions, wrestled with the questions, prayed his brokenness, and deepened the complexity of his faith. Perhaps he had to, if he were to choose to live again.

Andy stayed connected to his home church in Townsend, even though he was often at other churches on Sunday for worship. He continually looked for successful approaches that he could bring home. "Pub theology" caught his attention, and he decided to offer a study on the Lord's Prayer at a local restaurant, Bailey's Bar and Grille, in Townsend. He envisioned talking about faith with his neighbors over a beer. About a half dozen folks from various denominations met once a week for a month, thinking together about a familiar prayer, strengthening ecumenical linkages, and kindling conversations people assumed could happen only in church. He repeated this opportunity again years later.

Andy also provided a voice of calm and humor in decision-making. When the Townsend church wrestled with whether to widen its welcome, to publicly invite gay, lesbian, bisexual, and transgendered people to participate in their congregation, the pastor consulted Andy for advice. Andy gave one of those memorable answers that calm anxiety. "I don't think we should worry about that witness in the community. After all, anyone who truly loves Jesus and is actively engaged in serving the people of God is as queer as any lesbian, bisexual, gay, or transgender person who is in the church. Let's face it! Church people are queer. We shouldn't worry that gay people will make us queerer!" And soon thereafter, the church proclaimed a wider welcome.

Weaving Life's Strands

About that time, Andy's father, Leonard, had a stroke. Camping days ended as they stayed close to home. Andy's mother, Shirley, despite difficulty with her breathing, cared for her husband, aided by the West Brookfield Congregational Church and the extended family. Their daughter Karen and daughters-in-law Shelley and Carole developed a schedule, completed the tasks around the house, gave Shirley some respite, and offered company. Shirley, too, showed her age.

Andy and Carole wanted to do more for his parents. What if they could bring Leonard and Shirley to a cottage, to simulate camping again? When the Townsend Church held its fund-raising auction that year, Andy and Carole bid on a vacation at a cottage in northern Maine. They won and scheduled the trip. It was a long ride, but the cottage was right on the water. The porch's view enchanted them all, the bird calls woke them in the morning, and the smell of evergreens renewed their spirits. That memory sustained them for many months. Leonard died about a year later, in 2009.

Shirley lived alone, her dependence on bottled oxygen increasing. Carole, Shelley, and Karen spent more and more time in West Brookfield until they couldn't effectively care for her in this piecemeal fashion. Carole announced, "We're taking her home with us."

For a year, Shirley lived in the yellow colonial, slept in the library, and spent days in the living room. Some days she was well enough to cut apples for pie, but with her breathing needs supplied by the portable oxygen tanks, her basic life tasks often exhausted her energies. Still, she dreamed of seeing certain people and places one last time. So Andy and Carole responded by taking her to visit her sister on Cape Cod. The joy of that reunion delighted her for months in the remembering. It was the last time she would leave Townsend.

In the final months, Carole set up Shirley's hospital bed in the living room so she could be included in the family's life. On recalling this to me, Andy choked up as he spoke of his great appreciation for Carole's decision. "Carole brought her here and took care of whatever she needed. It meant I could be near my mother in those days and still do the job I loved. I am so grateful and blessed that this happened."

Although Bill May had served as a policeman in Townsend from 1974 and as chief from 1981 to 2002, even though he had responded to the 911 call and interrogated Andy, the two were not in relationship in the subsequent decades. Yes, if they passed each other at the town band concert, Andy would greet May by name, but little else. "It was awkward," May mused. "Neither of us knew how to deal with the memories, or the wrenching pain, inside and between us."

In 2012, now retired, May studied writing. He decided to write a memoir about police work in a small town, focusing on post-traumatic stress in emergency responders, victims of crimes, and people close to those who had been victimized. He intended this book to be helpful and healing to others and maybe to himself. May contacted people associated with two dozen of his cases, inviting them to tell their story. Andy was on that list.

When Chief May called, Andy listened deeply and prayed

about the possibilities. The vision of the book captured his heart. Certainly, this would be difficult, but the purpose of helping others, particularly those affected by trauma, motivated him to say yes. He had a story of post-traumatic growth and resilience to share.

The two met a half dozen times at Cliff's Cafe, across the common from the yellow colonial, before Andy drove to work in Framingham. In a corner booth, they caught up on news, ordered breakfast, and shifted to the book project. During the first meetings, they discussed the purpose of delving into the painful memories, how PTSD affected a multitude of people, how mental illness contributed to many crimes, how a book like this might be beneficial. Healing was the reason to dig again into this story; healing might come from such conversations. With that shared vision, they reconstructed the events of 1987 and 1988, a painstaking and emotional journey for both men. They reviewed the November robberies, the discovery of the murders, the manhunt, the police response. At times, both men cried. They talked honestly about how those events reverberated through time. May admitted his need to work through his own guilt. He feared he had exacerbated the pain of the murders with his extensive interrogation. May hoped for forgiveness, and Andy responded graciously. They moved beyond the crime, chronicling the funeral, his struggle with suicide, the spiritual turning points, and his choice to live a hope-filled, joyful life.

May later reflected, "He told me things straight from the heart. I was amazed by his strength and by his experience of God's grace. Did you know, he told me that God has a place for everyone? Do you know what I heard him saying? That God even has a place for someone like LaPlante." May remembered a quip Andy repeated from a seminary professor: "Christianity needs a hell, but you and I are not the ones to put anyone in it. Judgment belongs to God."

"Such courage, such faith," May, added, deeply moved.

When May completed a draft of *Once Upon a Crisis,* he brought it to Andy at the house. Andy sat in his recliner in the living room, quietly reading the manuscript while May fidgeted on the couch. Finishing, Andy sat silently for a long minute, but he didn't cry this time. Then, Andy looked up at the mantle with the angel figures of Cilla, Abby, and Billy. He smiled, took a deep breath, and turned to May. "Yes. Yes, this is OK to use."

The Gustafson family, circa 2009

Andy loved his daughters "to the moon and back." He had long been their champion, their cheerleader, and their ally. Holly and Laura grew into young women, graduated from high school, attended different colleges, and developed strong interests of their own. Carole and Andy celebrated Laura's studies at Mt. Wachusett Community College and Holly's accomplishments at Becker College in Leicester. With the Townsend house as home base, the daughters bounced from school to boyfriends' houses to places where they worked, back to home. It was the revolving-door stage of child development, the parents quipped. These changes felt disconcerting, but Andy learned another colleague was going through something similar. They batted around questions over coffee. "How is it to make space for an adult child? What rules and expectations make sense?" Typically, the conversations returned to the blessings each received by having the families close.

In May of 2012, the family celebrated Holly's graduation from nursing school and the start of her first professional job. Andy was so proud of her that his heart sang. Another life change took more adjustment. Laura was pregnant. She had a boyfriend, but they were not a stable couple. It turned out Andy was not alone in mulling over this situation, as he had a friend who had been presented with a parallel surprise. The two shared their feelings, often returning to humor. Through a mixture of excitement and confusion, joy and ambivalence, the unshakable core of love dominated.

In August 2012, Laura gave birth to a daughter. "It's official," Andy broadcast on Facebook. "I am a grandpa. Let me introduce you to Avari Rose." Laura's growth into motherhood impressed Andy. He told people how proud he was of his daughter. And how he enjoyed the role of grandfather, whether it was holding this beautiful newborn, watching her grow, reading her stories, laughing at her antics. He reveled in the daily ritual where he held Avari during dinner preparations. Granddaughter and grandfather bonded and gave each other life.

Grandpa Andy holds newborn Avari Rose, August 2012

Rarely did you see Andy's face more relaxed than when he was engaged with this little one. Avari was drawn to her grandpa Andy, bursting into smiles when she saw him, asking to be picked up, snuggling with him in his big easy chair, launching into the giggling that they shared. The role of grandparent fit Andy very well. But Avari brought another gift of deep healing. After Avari was born, Andy's still-residual crying spells, occasional nightmares, and slips into despair all seemed to disappear. It was like a miracle of new life. Another Easter.

On Patriot's day in 2013, a bomb exploded at the finish line of the Boston Marathon. With cameras already rolling for the sporting event, this act of terrorism unfolded in people's living rooms. How were people of faith to respond to it? Andy decided to write a blog, posted about a week later. It was an act of courage and love for those who would read this posting. Andy wrote,

> When tragedies happen, like happened in Boston this week, or in Newtown, it strikes us all very hard. It hits me very personally, especially when it involves children being murdered. It brings back memories of my own loss, when on December 1, 1987 my wife, Priscilla, and our two children, Abby who was a few days short of her eighth birthday and Billy who had just turned five, were murdered in our home by a young man we did not know, and for no apparent reason beyond the thrill of it. So I know grief, I know anger, I know the thirst for vengeance, I know darkness. But thanks to God, I also know the light shines in the darkness and that the darkness cannot overcome it.
>
> It is hard to make sense of the senseless. It may be impossible regardless of how much we try. We cherish life and seek to do whatever we can to make life better and

longer. But no matter what we do to reduce violence, to fight cancer, to make our highways safer, to eat healthier, all of which are good things, we still are not going to get out of this life alive. When faced with tragedy, whether it is personal or experienced collectively as we all have this last week, we are faced with a choice as to how we will respond: Will we let the darkness of hate infect our hearts, or will we choose to let perfect love cast out all fear? What I said at the funeral for my family is what I say to you this morning. The only fitting way to remember and honor those we have loved and lost is to live lives dedicated to love. I left the practice of law to work for the church to do my part in helping churches spread God's reign of love on earth.

The business of the church is love. That is the substance of our faith. The world needs us now more than ever. It needs our message of faith, hope and love. And that is the legacy we want to leave—a legacy of love.[11]

Andy testified to the Light, proclaiming the Gospel in the midst of violence and tragedy.

Sabbatical

One of the ways the church practices Sabbath is to offer its leadership a four-month sabbatical. Andy observed colleagues designing and enjoying their time away. His turn would happen in 2013. What did he want to do to recharge his batteries? Did he want to travel, to learn something new, to find Sabbath rest, to meet people he didn't know? What would help him rebalance his life for the next stage of ministry? Carole and Andy dreamed together for months.

Andy's work portfolio included coordinating the advanced planning for General Synod 30, the 2013 national meeting of the UCC church, to be held in Long Beach, California, the following June. Peter Wells happened to be in Framingham when the national office notified Andy that the Massachusetts delegation would be housed on the RMS Queen Mary. Andy and Peter let their imaginations loose, setting off an explosion of ideas and creative play that lit up the conference building. As Jim Antal told it, Andy and Peter's rumpus drew him out of his office as they swaggered down the hall, each with an eye covered with a patch, jabbering in pirate talk. "Aaaarg! A pirate theme for national meeting for me!" The announcement went out to all the delegates.

After many conversations, Andy decided he would focus his sabbatical on North America, exploring US national parks, visiting various churches, meeting people involved in mission projects, and connecting with friends he might not otherwise visit. He would attend the national church meeting in California, Synod. He delighted at planning the journey and laying it out so that he could arrive in Long Beach, California in late June to join his colleagues on the Queen Mary.

Remembering the game he played with Holly in elementary school, Andy created a sabbatical replacement, an image of himself, a Flat Andy, to sit in his bookshelf lined office in Framingham, to relax in his rolling chair, to stare out the windows at the flowers, to allow him to be in two places at once. At home, Carole created lists for Holly and Laura to use in managing the house. Andy and Carole drove south on Memorial Day weekend: across Connecticut, into New York and onto the New Jersey Turnpike. Andy preferred back roads, and soon they were headed for the Atlantic shore. As often happens with couples, Andy's and Carole's style of travel differed, and a three-month journey took some adjustments. Andy preferred to get up and get moving early, while Carole wanted a more leisurely, vacation pace. Negotiations were needed to be able to thread the needle between their preferences in those first days of the sabbatical journey.

Carole asked, "What time do you want to leave tomorrow morning?"

"I think eight would be a great time to get on the road," Andy replied, thinking it was decided. It isn't clear whether Carole actually said the perfunctory "all right" or whether she would remember these events differently. Either way, eight o'clock came and went without movement. Evidently, Andy was frustrated enough about this to make a comment in his blog. "This was one of those ceremonial exchanges which you know has no connection to reality. We left at 2:30 p.m. Love means living with stuff that really irritates you because the good stuff makes the irritating stuff seem meaningless."

That level of marital transparency never again appeared in his blog.

They traveled to mission sites helping to rebuild from Superstorm Sandy, to Kitty Hawk in honor of his love of flying, to historic Charleston, to Back Bay Mission near New Orleans. Weekly, they stopped to worship, sampling different kinds of music and levels of inclusion. On to San Antonio, Ft. Stockton, the Carlsbad Caverns, and Roswell, New Mexico, they drove. Andy seemed to cough more than usual, his stomach bothered him at times, and occasionally he noticed difficulty swallowing, but he attributed it to the change of climate and all the restaurant food. After all, they were having a wonderful time. The changing terrain caught Andy's attention, the different color pallet that contrasted with the landscape of New England. Andy blogged his love of Colorado, particularly Mesa Verde, the cliff dwellings that had been on his "bucket list" for years. He bubbled about the Grand Canyon and the beauty of high desert country with its different colors, plants and topography. He commented on some spectacular pictures of Antelope Canyon, "We aren't in Massachusetts anymore!"

The couple timed their travel perfectly, arriving at the national meeting, and taking up residence on the Queen Mary. The meeting itself was energetic, with colorful processions, lively music, important debates and votes, powerful preaching, and, of course, the pirate theme.

Andy in pirate dress on the Queen Mary at Synod, June 2013.

After five days of intense meetings, Andy and Carole relaxed at the San Diego Zoo. The journey then continued for another six weeks, starting with a trip across the Mexican border to a ministry of Centro Romero, in Tijuana that Andy found particularly impressive. Up the Pacific Coast they drove, visiting friends, touring Yosemite National Park, tasting wine in Napa Valley and enjoying the scenery of the Northwest. As they turned east, the car flashed a warning: service engine soon. Andy succeeded at getting more antacids and cough syrup, but failed at getting the car repaired. In a few miles, the engine emitted a high-pitched squeal. It was Saturday and they figured this meant a weekend in the middle of nowhere. To their surprise, they found a mechanics' shop open in Butte, Montana AND it had the part needed to fix the squeal. "God is good, all the time," they chanted to each other.

Andy deemed a day at Yellowstone National Park the best day of the Sabbatical. The video posted on Facebook of a buffalo saunter (as opposed to a stampede, he noted) that stopped traffic was classic Andy, with a running commentary of the most obvious nature. "Here is a buffalo coming toward us, there is one on the bank. My wife made me close the windows because she thought they might get in." Then, "I guess this is a buffalo migration, perhaps they are threatening civil disobedience," to which Carole quipped back, "Good thing there's a lawyer in the car."

Andy at the geysers of Yellowstone National Park, July 2013

They put two hundred miles on the car exploring Yellowstone, went through Jackson Hole, and continued through the Teton National Forest to a fun surprise on Carole's birthday, spotting a grizzly bear. That day finished with a dinner at a steak house with great local, seasoned beef, something that Andy prized, and thoroughly savored. It would be one of the last times he enjoyed such a good steak in a restaurant like this.

They traveled east, checking off many boxes on the bucket list—Mount Rushmore, the Wall Drug, the Corn Palace, Amish Country, and, back in Massachusetts, the Norman Rockwell museum.

Home again. Andy had planned two weeks to unpack, to camp, to reconnect with family and friends, to relax a bit before he would return to work at the Framingham conference office after Labor Day. He was glad he had.

It was August 2013 when Andy's and my story began to overlap.

The Short Term Pastor

When my phone rang in July of 2013, the moderator of the Townsend Congregational Church introduced herself to me and asked, "Reverend Waters, would you consider being the short-term pastor of our congregation? Our Area Minister Peter Wells suggested we consider a new type of pastor called a designated pastor, and we need someone for just a few months until we can find that person."

"Sure, tell me more," I replied.

Kathy and I talked for a long time, exploring the church's goals, discussing my skills and vision, reviewing their proposed time frame of three or four months.

"We'd like to interview you," Kathy said, "but we need to wait until Andy Gustafson gets back from sabbatical, mid-August. I'll call you to set up an appointment then." A couple of weeks later, we set the meeting for a Thursday in late August 2013.

The night of the interview, I parked across from the church and searched for an open door. Before I got far, Andy bounded out of the sanctuary, calling to me, welcoming me, and with a big laugh greeting me. "It's so good to see you! Come, let me show you my church."

We walked into the sanctuary, which was a bit dark and cool, but the evening light shone through the Good Shepherd stained glass window, the blue, white, and red glow creating a focal point for the whole room. Andy chattered. "It does get a bit hot here in the summer, so they run the fans when the windows are open. We have a really good music person, accomplished on the piano and the organ, and a very faithful choir."

Andy opened the door to the hallway and stopped, transfixed by the detailed woodcarving hanging in the hallway. He stared silently for a few moments, then, "Isn't this amazing? It's hand carved by one of our parishioners, a gift to celebrate the Resurrection. See the tomb here, the city of Jerusalem, the road to Emmaus, the sun rising." He paused, studying it. "We are so blessed to have this art work."

Then, as if the batteries started again, Andy bounded down the hallway. "Come see our Fellowship Hall. See how bright the room is, and air-conditioned, too. We are so proud of having this hall available for the whole town, a dream come true."

"It is impressive," I commented as we walked on.

"Yes, this was part of our capital campaign about ten years ago. And this elevator, too," he said, gesturing.

We meandered down the stairs. "This is the Congregational preschool. It serves children from newborn to early school age. I admire the director's creativity."

The three others on the interview committee met us in the hall, pointing the way to the conference room. When we sat down, Kathy introduced people around the table. She and Andy then started discussing their hopes for the church, the recent history, and the suggestion of using a limited rather than a nation-wide search for a pastor. I, as the temporary leader, would carry the pastoral responsibilities until the church found the designated pastor.

Andy, rocking back on his chair, cautiously described his perspective on the recent years and the healing he felt was needed. "I think this is something you would do well." He looked at me, smiled and tilted his head as he finished speaking.

After meeting with the team for an hour, I asked, a bit puzzled, "Do you have any questions for me?" I discovered I was the only candidate. We discussed start time, the likely ending date, the nature of three-quarter-time employment and the focus of my short stint in Townsend. Andy explained that he would be returning to his work in Framingham in September and would not be around most Sundays; however, he would continue to be the assistant moderator and available as a sounding board to me, as needed. It was a great beginning.

I started my covenant in Townsend the Tuesday after Labor Day. The following Saturday, a group of Townsend members gathered at the home of the Sunday School superintendent to talk about programming. My GPS located the street off the main road, but finding a place to park was challenging. There were a dozen cars and vans parked up and down the narrow road, and the driveway was marked, "For turning around only." I ended up parking a quarter of a mile away.

Finding the door open, I wandered through the house to the back yard where a picnic party was in full swing, with children running around, teens bringing more food, a man overseeing the grill and a cooler full of drinks to welcome one and all. One of the search committee members called out, "It's so good you are here!" and took me around to be introduced. I spotted Andy with a straw hat sitting in a plastic chair, quiet, somewhat pensive, drinking a soda, and listening to those around him. The Sunday School superintendent got everyone's attention. "The first round of hot dogs and hamburgers is coming off the grill and there are lots of other dishes here to share. It would be great if people would come get their plates and then gather in a circle." After the commotion around the food table, a big circle sprouted on the grass. Andy's voice invited people into the conversation circle.

The superintendent led introductions and detailed plans for children and youth. Andy applauded the programs and expressed excitement about the confirmation class. He wondered about additional special activities focused on youth, perhaps teaming with neighboring churches.

That Sunday, I preached, Sunday School began, and a cake welcomed people back from vacation. Andy and Carole sat in their typical side pew, chatting with others before church, offering up prayers of thanksgiving in worship. During coffee hour, they greeted people they hadn't seen since their return from sabbatical. Andy, his new ten-gallon cowboy hat fashionably askew on his bald head, could be spotted from across the room. Most of the time, he stood with small groups, listening intently, chatting with hand gestures, but his smile and laughter were less evident than I remembered in other settings. I heard him cough several times and wondered if he had a cold. There were times when he stood alone sipping his coffee. I felt that something was not right, even when he brushed off my, "How are you?" with, "Fine. Making the transition back to work is harder than I expected."

Over the next few weeks, Carole hinted at something more. "Andy's health isn't quite right," she confided. "He has difficulty eating and swallowing. He coughs a lot, but he resists checking it out."

Andy returned to his customary routine. He attended Cabinet meetings once or twice a month on Wednesdays at supper-time. As we considered goals for the short-term pastorate, Andy wondered if I could lead the congregation in answering the question, "Do we want to revitalize our church?" He felt the congregation had been pushed to a level of change that brought resistance. If they could freely choose and feel some unity, he mused, perhaps that would set the course for going forward. Sure, I said, great goal.

Now that Andy was back at work in Framingham, Flat Andy retired to a closet and large-tall Andy filled the conference center with laughter and constant chattering from his office, even when he was alone. He found many opportunities to support pastors and congregations, on the phone, in person, at local churches. One pastor posted on Facebook her joy in a "fabulous theological conversation about money and giving" with Andy. With members of various boards Andy put final touches on a new proposal to replace membership dues. The roll-out would start with the county leadership committees.

In addition, Andy needed to sift through the four-month backlog of emails and paper mail, prepare for lay learning events, attend the Board Meeting of Worcester Fellowship, and set up visits and preaching at a multitude of churches. Andy's difficulty with his eating, swallowing, and choking continued, but he brushed it off as acid reflux and kept thinking it was getting better, or would, once the stress of readjusting settled down.

An all-church decision-making group, meeting at the Townsend church, quickly agreed to the limited search for a pastor. But then, unscripted, a member of the choir stood to challenge the previous May's decision to reduce the staff positions, to eighty-five percent of their time and money. Evidently, the choir rose to defend their director. "We want our leader to return to her previous number of hours with full pay." The moderator was quick to reply. "That topic will need another meeting, announced for that purpose."

Then came the news. The moderator had breast cancer. It had been caught early; the reports were filled with hope. Nevertheless, Andy, as assistant moderator, accepted more responsibility for the council, and organized the all-church meeting reviewing the previous decision to reduce staff time and money. That evening's meeting gathered about two dozen church members, of whom three quarters were, or had been, choir members. The church treasurer took the lead, reviewing the reasoning cited for reducing positions and proposing that if the money could be raised to fund this reinstatement—about five thousand dollars––then she would support their desires to return non-pastoral staff to 100% of their contracts.

Andy took a different tack. Moving to the center of the room, he began to speak—no, preach, really. His rhythms, his changing tone, his passion, carried the group as a singer would draw in a crowd. This community knew his story, shared the tragedy, walked with him in choosing life, and responded to his spiritual leadership.

"What we do as a church, it's important." Andy preached. "What we do is important to the people here, to the town, to the children, to the children not yet born. What we do here is nourish the Light, the Light that is proclaimed on that cemetery stone just over that hill," Andy gestured broadly. "We shine God's Light, the Light that shines in the darkness, together. We must. It matters. What we do matters to the world."

I, along with the rest of the people, sat transfixed, covered with goose bumps. As Andy returned to his seat, check books popped out of purses and back pockets. The next Sunday, the treasurer announced that she had received enough to reinstate all support staff with some left for the beginning of 2014.

Is it Cancer?

By mid-October, Andy was coughing more and had increasing difficulty eating and swallowing. In addition, he was experiencing intense bouts of pain across his chest. Carole knew this and kept nagging him to make an appointment. Finally he did, scheduling it for early November. In the meantime, Andy continued to work, ignoring the pain as much as possible: visiting churches around the conference, bringing mirth to his fellow staff, working in the kitchen for the church suppers, choosing a Halloween pumpkin with granddaughter Avari.

The first doctor's appointment raised more questions than it answered. It could be a hernia, it could be acute GERD, it could be something more serious, even cancer. Now came the specialists, the tests, the endoscopy, the waiting. At first the news was vague. Carole became more creative in adapting his menus—smoothies, soups, meat cut extra fine. Just after Thanksgiving, I heard a more specific report. The results pointed toward the answer no one wanted to hear, cancer. I arranged a visit for the next day.

Walking down the street from the church, past the jeep and well-used car, over the eroded driveway, up the uneven path to the wooden steps, I lifted up my anxiety to God. I opened the outside door into the anteroom, a room with baby formula and soda bottles piled on the bench, unsure whether I had chosen the right entry. My knock was answered with fierce barking and a sharp,

"Stop that!" The door opened into a small kitchen, daughter Laura restraining a lunging boxer by the collar, a dog with one bulging, blood shot eye. "This is Hunter. Don't mind him, he's old and deaf. We'll put him behind the gate."

Carole and I hugged, and she pointed to the next room. "Go in." Andy stood to greet me and we exchanged a lingering hug. I perched on the couch across from him. The small room held a his-and-her recliner, a TV, a sofa, some extra chairs, a coffee table, and some side tables piled with papers and books. As we chatted, Andy gestured to a high mantel covered with small figurines underneath a half-moon window. "Those are my angels, my first family. They are always close by."

I smiled. I knew this story only vaguely. I would go home that night and Google to find more information.

"I heard you had difficult news," I opened.

"Yes, but there are still more tests. The MRI is this week, but results will take longer."

There was a silence. When he spoke again, his voice tightened and he fought back tears. "If it is stage four, I think I won't fight. I will go and join Cilla and the children," pointing to the mantel.

We both were silent for a few moments, then we explored his feelings, how his daughters were taking the news, how he felt God's presence in the midst of this time of waiting.

"It's Advent," I reflected.

"It's Advent," he smiled. "Yes, waiting."

"Would you like to invite family and friends to pray with and for you, to lay hands on you? Maybe here or at the church?" I asked.

His face brightened. "I would really like that. Yes, at church."

"I will make an announcement, and you can invite the people that you would really like to be there. I hope your daughters will come."

Shaking his head doubtfully, "I'm not sure they will." His head dropped. "They aren't into church very much."

"Just let them know they are welcome. And if they want to talk, I will be glad to meet with them." I replied.

As our visit drew to a close, I invited Carole into the room and we prayed together.

The word of Andy's diagnosis spread quickly: esophageal cancer. As we gathered for the second Sunday of Advent, lighting candles for peace, singing our hope, speaking our longing for change, Andy and Carole held hands in the side pew. After worship and coffee fellowship, their daughters slipped into Fellowship Hall. I announced that we would come together for healing prayer in five minutes here in this big room, to accommodate the crowd.

I placed two chairs in the middle of the space, invited Andy and Carole to sit, and motioned to Laura and Holly to choose where they would stand. Then I invited participants to place their hands on Andy or Carole, or on someone who was touching them. The crowd made a circle, with people flowing out into the hallway. I explained the process: first silent prayer, then I would pray aloud, then invite silent or spoken prayers from group members.Then I would draw us to a close and finish with the Lord's Prayer.

The room became deeply silent, some people cried, some repeated prayers under their breath, some shifted their feet, a bit uncomfortable with the process. I began with words, calling on the Holy Spirit to be with us, asking for Jesus' healing, comfort, strength, and peace, thanking God for the blessings and courage he had already bestowed on Andy and his family, and praising the Triune God's power, grace, and mercy so integral to Andy's life. The group offered inspired, heart-felt prayers from many voices, some speaking a short time, some longer. The Holy Spirit pulsed in the room, abundant love flowed freely, silent hope of healing grew stronger, and faith unified the group with the words of the Lord's Prayer. Andy smiled as he walked home.

Carole and Andy were ready to share their news publicly. Carole did so with this post on Facebook.

"Andy was just diagnosed with malignant esophageal cancer that has probably been growing since a year ago November. He had an endoscopy and they took a biopsy. It is rather large and constricting the esophagus. Eating is difficult and he has been on liquids and smooth, slippery foods. Went for a cat scan Friday and will see the chief of the gastrointestinal clinic at Dana-Farber tomorrow, late morning. We should know more then. He started having difficulty eating with a pain across his chest in late October. Prior to that he had some bad reflux. Over the years he has taken Pepcid to combat minor bouts but nothing outrageous. Never a smoker. We are trying to remain positive and hopeful, but it has thrown us for a loop. December already brought sadness with the death of my first husband from a brain tumor and the murder of his family. Thankfully the spirit of Christmas brightens the darkness....... If you have prayer warriors please enlist them."

As they waited for news, they researched this cancer. If it were stage one, where the cancer cells were contained, surgery might be an option. A member of the congregation had had stage one esophageal cancer, treated with surgery and a feeding tube. It took a long time to heal, but now he was doing OK. Yes, he was an esophageal cancer survivor, now thin and frail, but alive.

Since it was December, Andy wanted to find an event that would kindle the Christmas spirit. They found that in Portsmouth, N.H., Charles Dickens's great-great grandson was offering a one-man rendition of Dickens' "Christmas Carol." That was it! They decided to go. When they got there, unable to manage a typical meal, they bought some soup at a local stand. It tasted good. Andy ate some slowly, then somehow spilled about half the cup. He decided he had had enough and ate no more. It was an enjoyable evening, but he was exhausted when he returned and chose not to attend church the next day.

The following week, Andy and Carole, bundled against the cold, celebrated the outdoor nativity play put on by the children and youth of Townsend Congregational Church, sipping hot cider, and participating in conversation in the warmth of the hall following the event. They were excited to have so many children and families involved. "This is my hope and vision for this congregation," Andy whispered to me.

It snowed, and both Carole and Andy encouraged their daughters to shovel. There was some initial rebellion, but the job finally got done. Andy missed the Framingham staff party because of yet another doctor's appointment, so Flat Andy made an appearance in the photo shoot. The good news—Flat Andy didn't eat all the shrimp cocktail; the bad news—Flat Andy didn't fill the room with laughter either.

On Christmas Eve, Andy attended the 10:00 p.m. candlelight service, sitting in the back row, slipping in late and leaving quickly. We did catch a hug, a Merry Christmas and best wishes, but I noticed that he had lost some weight.

Carole simplified the traditional Christmas plans, omitting the party that gathered the diverse branches of the extended family. There was a beautiful tree and presents, especially for Avari. Watching the toddler's delight brightened everyone's mood. The whole family traveled to the traditional dinner with Larry and Shelley in South Hadley. Andy, upbeat and enjoying the festivities, did what he always did. He reached for the shrimp, unconsciously took a bite, and tried to swallow. The bite started to go down, but then stopped, as food would do in those days. He choked, he gagged, he gasped for breath, he cried out in pain, the private reality unveiled for all to see. When he discharged the piece of shrimp and the panic subsided, sadness engulfed the room. Andy loved to eat and now he couldn't.

Carole worked hard to make things Christmassy, making Andy a smoothie with eggnog and ice cream for him to sip. Shelley invited Andy to watch football in the living room while everyone else ate roast beef in the dining area. "Wait," said Andy. "Can I smell the roast beef before I go?"

"Of course," came the reply. Andy lingered over a slab of the juicy, rare meat and then adjourned with his drink. There was holiday spirit and a heaviness of worry; they were happy to be together as a family, and sad that Andy was not himself.

The Treatment Plan

Two days after Christmas, procedures and tests meant a whole day at Dana-Farber in Boston, but ultimately it seemed worth it. On the eve of Andy and Carole's 25th wedding anniversary, December 31, 2013, they heard the first test results: positive news. The main cancer was contained, with just a couple of little spots elsewhere to investigate. Likely stage one, but they needed to check the three tiny spots that lit up away from the main tumor.

The New Year dawned and everyone wanted to get back to normal. Andy went to work, but came home early with a sore back. It snowed more, and this time the daughters shoveled without any coaching or complaining.

When I came to visit that first week of January, Andy had a different kind of news to share. "Tom Reilly, from the District Attorney's office, called," he began. "A week or two ago, the Massachusetts Supreme Court ruled that inmates given life without parole sentences while a juvenile, must now be considered for a parole." He took a long pause. "That means Daniel LaPlante could get released. I think I am going to write a letter to the parole board."

We sat in silence for a while. I asked what I thought was a pastoral question. "Do you want to do any forgiveness work?" Andy answered with a sharp and curt, "No!" We never talked about it again, but I certainly thought about it, especially in writing this testimony. Did I not acknowledge all the forgiveness work that had already happened? There is no doubt that he had been on the forgiveness journey for decades. He had not let these events paralyze finding new life. He had turned the power of his emotions in a positive direction—advocating for youth like Daniel in the court, and bringing his experiences to theological reflection in the face of violence. He had embodied the way God works to overcome darkness in his words and deeds. He had dared to live joyfully and with gratitude, and invited others to do likewise. He had even avoided condemning Daniel directly, leaving to God the decision about forgiveness. Was I wrong to ask the question? Was it the wrong timing with the possibility of Daniel's release, with his decision to advocate for continued incarceration, in order to protect others from more violence if he were to be released? What is forgiveness and is it ever finished?

The second week in January, Carole and Andy met with the oncologist to review and synthesize all the test findings: the MRI's, the endoscopy, the blood work, the pathology reports. They had been holding their breath for six weeks, waiting for this meeting. They drove to the appointment through stormy weather, parked, and anxiously waited for the conclusive diagnosis, hoping, praying for stage one. When the doctor pointed to the spot on the back, and reported further tests showed no cancer cells, their hope grew. But the doctor's expression turned more serious as he pointed near the kidney. "These results do show cancer cells, here on the adrenal glands. I'm so sorry." No one wanted these results. The pathology report shifted the diagnosis from stage one to stage four, with the accompanying alteration in prognosis. Andy and Carole never shared with me what they were told, but a nurse in the congregation came to me to explain her understanding: six months, if they are lucky.

What I heard about was the doctor's more positive proposal: treatment. With recent advances in drug treatment and Andy's relative youth, good general health, and great attitude, the doctor recommended a course of chemo and radiation to kill the cancer cells, and aid in swallowing. Surgery was off the table for now. They decided that Dana-Farber's outreach site at Concord's Emerson Hospital would be the place to receive this treatment while retaining the main doctors in Boston.

When I met with Andy next, both he and Carole were set for the battle, and any thoughts of declining treatment were long gone. Carole put it this way. "We are not giving up and will continue to battle, for miracles do happen. God might be getting tired of all the intercessions She has been getting and let that miracle come to pass." After all, Greg had lived two and half years on a six-month prognosis and Andy had fought his way to new life overcoming what seemed insurmountable odds. Fighting made total sense to Carole, and in those conversations, Andy reinvested completely in his life. Hope took hold.

The six-week course of treatment would begin mid January. The forty-five minute drive six days a week with radiation every day and additional time for chemo once a week would demand most of the energy available, so Andy hatched a plan. He wanted to go cross-country skiing now. Actually, he'd been thinking about this since it started to snow in December, but he couldn't find his ski boots.

"Who's seen my ski-boots? I'm sure I put them right here."

"Don't know, Dad," came the reply from two rooms away.

Andy rustled through the bucket of winter gear, peered in his closet, searched the garage, and hunted in the basement. No luck.

He began to grouse, "Which one of you took them? I always keep them in the winter box." No luck.

Finally a few days after radiation began, Andy found them—in a pile of his own stuff. Yes, he'd looked in that area before, but not deeply and thoroughly enough. Something brought him back to this place and, as if returned by elves, the boots were right there for him to find. He wrote on Facebook, "On discovering them I felt just like the woman in the parable who found the lost coin after scouring her house. And so I praise God and rejoice—that which was lost is found!"

The next day, Andy cross-country skied through Howard Park, breaking a trail through newly fallen snow. He shared his blessing on Facebook. "The snow was still on the trees and bushes, and it was incredibly beautiful. I find getting out in nature, whether on skis, hiking or in a kayak, is not only good physically and mentally, but also renews my spirit. I feel connected to that other part of God that is present and visible in all creation."

This was a time of promise, possibility, and gratitude. "I have been through my first two treatments of radiation," he wrote, "and my first chemo and feel fine. I know over time the effects will be cumulative, but so far so good. Knowing I am being held in prayer by so many is a great source of comfort and strength, as is my knowledge of God's presence and love and the cloud of witnesses who surround me," (Hebrews 12:1).

Carole constantly supported Andy, driving him to appointments, fixing him drinks and soft food, encouraging his efforts to do what work he could. Other reinforcements appeared as well. A church friend, who works for a dairy, brought the beloved eggnog before it disappeared from store shelves. Another delivered a case of Ensure. The conference staff sent weekly messages and small gifts: photos of Flat Andy, get well cards, gift cards for gas, coupons to buy food at the Emerson cafeteria, a gift certificate to Gibbets Grill. Friends came to visit, play cards, watch a sports game on TV or bring food. Andy and Carole never failed to talk about the blessings showered upon them in the midst of this cancer battle.

Radiation treatments lasted thirty minutes from beginning to end. There turned out to be another Townsend UCC church member also receiving radiation, although she didn't want people at

Flat Andy taken by Conference Staff in Framingham to cheer
Andy's spirits

the church to know. They cheerfully greeted and encouraged each
other day after day. Chemo day once a week stretched to four
hours. I asked about hanging out with Andy on a chemo day, but
our next visit was still held at his house. The church council had
sent me on a mission.

Andy greeted me, sharing his excitement about the recent Patriot's win, and asking questions about church business. We discussed what he wanted people to pray for, and the prayer concerns
of others in the church. He described the conference work he was
tackling from home, but then shook his head. "I have so much
more to do."

"You have wonderful gifts to share. The conference needs
them," I encouraged.

I knew, however, that today I would ask him to step down
as assistant moderator and to invite him to find a replacement. I
approached this gingerly, aiming to keep hope growing, but also
dealing realistically with the responsibilities of the church.

"Andy," I ventured. "The council talked at our last meeting. We think it might be a good idea, until you get back on your feet, to find someone to fill the role of Assistant Moderator."

"I'm going to get better," he asserted.

"I hope and pray that will be so. God can do amazing things. But, you will need healing time before your full energy returns. With such a small council, we need everyone's effort. We hope you can help fill the position, think of a person who would fit this role well and ask them. We would welcome you back to leadership as soon as you are able."

He paused for a few moments. "You are probably right. Let me think about it."

When I talked with Andy a week later, he told me that he had called Lynn, a person who had been less active for a while, but who was ready to re-engage. He and Lynn talked, and she agreed to take on the role. Andy's insight and influence continued to mentor leadership that might not have happened without him.

Chemo and Radiation

I scheduled visiting with Andy during his treatment, but a snow-storm canceled the first date. Peter Wells came from western Massachusetts to spend the treatment time with him the following week. As usual, when these two got together, they caught people's attention, their raucous banter entertaining the whole unit. It was a hard act to follow.

The next week, using Carole's directions, I arrived at Emerson Hospital's cancer unit. Coming in, I met a parishioner. She told me that she had been the one receiving radiation at approximately the same time as Andy, but that she didn't want those at the church to know. We hugged and chatted. She had battled cancer before. The doctors had caught the reemergence of cells early, and expected treatment would lead to remission again. When we finished our conversation, she pointed the way up the stairs to the chemo center.

The signs led to the check-in window. I told the receptionist my purpose, and walked to the waiting area, a larger room with a wall of windows, sets of chairs by magazine-covered tables, a bowl of knitted hats with a "Take One" sign, and one person sitting by himself in a corner. In a few minutes, Carole came out to greet me.

"How's he doing today?" I asked.

"Pretty well. The hydration perks him up and he seems to be handling the chemo OK."

I nodded.

"He's looking forward to your visit. I'll walk you in and then come back to the waiting room. There isn't a lot of extra room back there."

I entered an elongated room with windows on two sides. There were six beige vinyl recliners positioned near the windows, white boards on the wall across from them, and a couple of cheerful attendants going from person to person. Andy reclined at the same angle he enjoyed at home, with three different intravenous bags pumping chemicals and fluids into his body.

"Good to see you," I began.

Andy laughed and smiled. "I'm really glad you're here."

The nurse came by to check the drip bags hanging on the rack, making sure the tubes leading to a semi-permanent implanted shunt flowed well. "Doing OK?" she asked.

Andy nodded.

"Session four today?" I was trying to be encouraging.

"Yes, two more to go."

We chatted about the process of searching for the new pastor at church, his daughters and my sons, his frustrations about not being able to do the work for the conference, about upcoming plans for Lent. There were a few snowflakes dancing outside the windows. After almost two hours, Carole came in.

"Lunch?" she asked. We looked at the menu and I pull out my wallet. "Don't worry," she said, "I have this gift card for lunches here. I'll pay for it."

We ate together in the treatment room, the dripping chemicals slowly flowing into Andy's body. Although we did not name it aloud, each of us pinned our hopes on that chemo cocktail stopping the rampage of the unwanted cells. We finished lunch. Andy's drip bags completed their cycle and the nurse came by to do the finishing steps. We prayed together and said goodbye.

Carole walked out with me. "So, how is it going at home?" I

asked.

"I'm really tired," she confessed. "And the drives back and forth are getting tougher. He gets nauseous, especially on the trips home."

"I'm so sorry. Have you talked to the doctor about that?"

"No, I guess we should."

We hugged. "Let me know if there is anything I can do."

We looked out the window to see heavy snow.

"Drive carefully," Carole called.

"You, too," I responded.

For the first several weeks of treatment, Andy showed few side effects from the bombardment of radiation and chemo drugs, but by the end of February, his strength had declined and his walk had slowed. After only a few minutes on his feet, his gait regressed to a shuffle. Now Carole would drop him off by the door rather than have him walk from the parking lot. Still, his spirit was strong and he spoke often of his confidence in healing. At his last chemo treatment February 26, as is the tradition on the unit, Andy rang the bell, smiling ear to ear.

March began with a time of rest and waiting. Andy and Carole talked about doing something different, perhaps a trip to Florida to stay with Andy's sister. Carole remembered traveling with Greg and how renewing it was for all of them. They needed a change of scenery, some warm weather that would allow them to get outside, some distance from all the doctors' visits. The doctors doubted that Andy would be ready and able, but Carole decided to book the trip anyway.

Andy began having more trouble swallowing the smoothies and soups. His discomfort, his gagging, his difficulty getting hydrated and the challenge of taking in enough calories meant he was experiencing more pain than he communicated. He kept focusing on hope, on gratitude, on blessings. His friends and family provided much companionship and distraction. On St. Patrick's Day, as the Gustafsons shared corned beef and cabbage with friends, Andy ate his beef cut into the tiniest pieces one could imagine.

I visited regularly. One time in late March, I brought materials that would be distributed through the town, inviting people to our Holy Week events. Andy and I met in the family library that day, a small room lined with bookcases and stacked with papers. He tried to stand as I entered, but it was clearly difficult and I motioned for him to stay seated. Carole had told me that mornings were getting much more difficult, the walk downstairs tediously slow. Andy rarely moved during the day except to use the toilet. I could see his pallor, his reduced energy, and his weakening ability to focus. But when I showed him the brochures, his energy lifted, and tears began to flow. "This," he exclaimed, "this is just what I hoped could happen for our congregation, for our community for Holy Week." He was so grateful that I had brought the materials for him to see, to celebrate, to praise God. That day, he led the prayer when we finished, the first time in many weeks that he had spoken while we prayed together.

Throughout the month of March, he lost more weight, and his clothes hung on his body. He needed thinner and thinner liquids to prevent choking, and even getting enough water was difficult. Carole believed that intravenous hydration boosted his energy and improved his coloring for a day or two. She pushed for more frequent hydration than the medical people recommended. Originally, the cancer team planned to wait for two months after

Andy and Avari March 2014

treatment before repeating the MRI, but with Andy's increasing difficulty swallowing, another endoscopy was ordered.

They postponed the trip to Florida.

The reports on the endoscopy came back with encouraging news. The evaluator reported that stiffness was caused by the radiation rather than by cancer intruding into the esophagus. They prescribed a dilation of the esophagus. Andy's hope rose as he posted on Facebook, "If all goes well at Brigham & Women's on Friday, the esophageal dilation will allow me to eat (relatively) normally again for the first time in six months. Having lost 50 lbs I am looking forward to putting a few back on."

The first dilation stretched his esophagus to about eight millimeters, enough for thin liquids, not what Andy had envisioned. He wrote on Facebook, "The great news is that yesterday's procedure revealed no cancer in my esophagus. The radiation and chemo and prayers did their work. The disappointment is that because my esophagus is so narrowed, the dilation could only open it up so much in one treatment without risking a tear, so I am still only able to drink thin fluids. I go back next week for another dilation and hopefully, I will be able to start eating after that one. I want to thank everyone for their prayers and support."

Andy's post set off a flurry of joy and hope. Many heard this message as "Andy is cancer free," and anticipated his return to his old job and his old self, but my visits did not match this perception. What I saw was continual decline. At the meeting of the executive board of the Central Association, I felt unsure of how to handle a conversation with this interpretation.

"Did you hear that Andy was cancer free?" said one of the members.

What does a pastor say to something like that? There is confidentiality and there is what is public. I decided to emphasize what was specifically said on Facebook. "The post said there was no cancer in the esophagus. For that I am grateful, but he isn't well yet. We need to keep praying."

I hoped that I made the right call.

At home, Andy's frustration grew because eating, which he so loved, was impossible now. His hope lay in a future where he could eat solid food again, but could he stay strong enough to heal? They talked of a feeding tube, but Andy resisted. He knew there would be a cost, a setback as well as a gain, if they put in a tube and bypassed the esophagus.

Andy wanted the second dilation to be scheduled for the next week, sooner than the medical establishment preferred to do it. They struck on a compromise of ten days. This time, the procedure gained another two millimeters, enlarging the esophagus to ten millimeters, about half of normal. But what really made Andy choke was the doctor's response to his question, "When will I be able to eat solid food again?"

"I'm sorry, Andy," came the reply. "I do not think you will ever be able to eat solid food. I don't know how much wider we can safely and effectively dilate this part of your body."

Now, Andy showed open anger at home. He got angry at the coughing, angry at being hungry, angry that he couldn't have the foods he longed for, angry at not being able to work and do what he had imagined. Anger thrust outward in sharp words, in grousing, in a raised voice, in a hardened and glum face. Anger turned inward to depression, deep sighs, less willingness to talk, and an air of resignation. Carole and his daughters felt his emotions most fully.

Friday night, at church, a storyteller enchanted about two dozen listeners. Carole, who noted that she really needed to get out of the house by herself for a while, was delighted at the tales, especially the story about a salesman who dealt with his anger by smashing windows in his basement. That story provided the metaphor of communication between Carole and me in the next weeks. "How many windows did you smash today?" I would text. She could tell me her experience living through Andy's strong but understandable anger, even though it was difficult for her to endure.

On Tuesday of Holy Week, Carole drove Andy to the Framingham office as a surprise. When the staff heard his distinctive voice and laughter, they all bolted out of their offices to join the festivities. The place bubbled with joy; they felt whole again that afternoon. In the short stay, he spoke with everyone. Near the end, the whole group encircled him and they prayed together, with tears welling up in many eyes. The staff also saw the reality—the pain in Andy's back flashing across his face, quickly replaced by the laughter and smiles that so characterized his coping style. After the Gustafsons headed back to Townsend, the staff hugged each other, sharing their fears and surprise at Andy's thin, frail body and his difficulty walking. They also celebrated Andy's continued determination and joyful presence, on which they all relied.

"Andy's Not Doing Well"

Andy longed to participate in some of the events planned for Holy Week, but he did not have the energy. It was a major battle to get from his bedroom to the living room once a day. Attending Easter worship became his goal. Easter morning, I received a text message from Carole. "Could you save seats for us at the rear of the sanctuary?" I found two reserved signs, placed them in the back pew, and texted back, "Done."

At the beginning of worship, the seats were empty, and I sighed. The music rose from the choir, the trumpet sounded and the congregation's voices swelled, singing, "Christ the Lord is Risen Today! Alleluia!" During the second verse, Andy slowly and laboriously moved from the stairs to the pew and sat. My eyes filled with tears. Andy worshipping with us was my Easter. Throughout worship, through prayers and scriptures, through hymns and anthems, I felt my heart leap with joy at Andy's presence, understanding the sacrifice it took for him to be here, experiencing the love this congregation had for him, and he for them.

I recessed to the back of the church with the final, "Thine Is the Glory," raised my hand to offer the benediction, and began to sing the congregational blessing. As Andy stood to go, I greeted and hugged Carole and him, knowing they needed to leave because all their energy had been spent. He stooped, with little ability to lift his feet, flashed a smile, and said,

"He is Risen."

"Risen, indeed," I responded. Then, carefully and slowly, they descended the few steps to the walkway and were off to share Easter dinner with his brother in the Amherst area. That would be the last time Andy would attend worship here, and somehow, I knew that.

The following week, as they waited for the check-up planned for the beginning of May, Andy continued to wither and to shudder with pain. His friends suggested a soak in their hot tub, which he accepted, enjoying every moment. The friends lifted him up and put him on his feet when he finished, and Carole drove him home.

May brought another clinic appointment for hydration, stronger pain medication, and conversations about a feeding tube. The doctor set the PET scan as a higher priority and moved up the schedule to the upcoming Monday in Boston, with a follow-up appointment to interpret the results the next day.

That first Sunday in May the Central Association held its Annual Meeting. Near the end of the gathering, I leaned over to the conference minister and whispered, "Andy's not doing well." She whispered back, "Call the office in Framingham. Call Jim (the Conference President). They need to know."

I knew there was an important doctor's appointment on Tuesday that would give more information, but I decided to call my contact at the conference office, Andy's administrative assistant, Monday morning to communicate my concern. The Conference President, Jim, called me back.

"It doesn't look good to me," I offered. "I think it would be timely if you went to see him soon. They have this appointment tomorrow. I will tell Carole and Andy I've called you, and see what they say, especially after the appointment."

Andy's brother Larry drove them to Boston that Monday, a day originally scheduled for another dilation, a day that would turn out to be long and difficult as they learned that the esophagus had closed up because a tumor pressed against it. Overpowered by his pain, drained by moving to the various doctors' appointments, exhausted of any reserve of energy, Andy needed to stop, to find a space to rest, to receive intravenous hydration and nutrition, to find medication to relieve his suffering. In the end, he checked into Brigham and Women's Hospital. Larry drove Carole home, and she returned in her car the following morning.

On Tuesday, they heard the results of the PET scan. It was the worst-case scenario. Andy's body was rife with cancer—in his pelvis, back, neck, liver, and brain. The shock, depression, and confusion stunned them. But Carole did what Carole had always done best, she accompanied Andy every step of the way. She settled into the chair that transformed into a cot by the window in Andy's small private hospital room on the twelfth floor of the Brigham. Side by side, they listened to the doctors, talked when they could, and appreciated being in each other's presence.

When I came to visit, traversing the many corridors of this complex, I found Andy's room in a set of doors encircling the nurses' station. The small space had enough room for the bed, the variety of machines, one folding chair, one side chair, and a door to a bathroom. I often stood against the wall as the stream of practitioners flowed in and out of the room. Almost as soon as I arrived, a crew came to plan the next round of radiation. As I listened to Carole and Andy catch me up on what was happening, I heard the vision of another six months. It didn't seem realistic to me, but I wasn't a doctor.

They put in a feeding tube, balanced his hydration and electrolytes, found the right pain medication, walked with him in the hallway, and started the radiation. The first few days in the hospital, Andy's color, his focus, and his hopefulness improved.

During our visits, Andy repeated his concern that he had more to give. How could God not value his work, knowing his passion for the church? I had heard this concern since December, but here, in May, Andy still worried about things left undone. We talked about letting go, about trusting that others would carry on. I mentioned all the resources he had already developed and the many people he had trained to be stewards. We were acknowledging, although not yet directly, that the end of life was approaching.

I let Conference President Jim Antal know of this work concern still active in Andy's mind. Andy and Carole traded emails with the conference office, setting up a time for Jim to visit. He arranged a schedule for the rest of the Framingham office staff to come to the hospital, to boost Andy's spirit by sharing love and laughing together.

Over the next days, Andy and Carole spoke with multiple oncologists and radiologists—his primary cancer doctor and the one who inserted the stomach tube, the specialists focused on the shoulder and the one who would irradiate his brain. Each presented an aggressive plan for fighting the cancer. They started the radiation on the shoulder, but Andy found the pain of being transported, the tedium of the wait, the intrusion of being awakened in the night, overwhelming. He and Carole envisioned the plan proposed to irradiate the brain, the fifteen drives from Townsend to Emerson, the task of moving from the house to the car to the hospital without help, the treatment's possible damage to his thinking. The plan seemed excruciating. When I visited, we talked about the quality of life, about God's leadings, about using the time left wisely.

The hospice team offered the greatest peace. That team worked with his pain and painted a vision of moving forward without additional treatment, while living each moment. It took a couple of days, but finally Andy and Carole chose hospice. They stabilized nutrition with a feeding tube, learned the right medication mix to manage pain, stopped all aggressive treatment, and made the arrangements to go home with hospice services.

People visited the hospital. Andy and a former pastor talked of the Kingdom of God. A friend from the Cape visited and reminisced about their lives in Townsend. Peter Wells' arrival brought laughter and tears. Laura and Avari came, sitting at the bedside, holding hands, and taking some of the last pictures of grandfather, granddaughter, and daughter.

About a week after Carole and Andy began living in the small hospital room, people back in Townsend wanted to help, wanted to prepare the house for their return. After much cajoling, Carole gave permission to a bevy of friends who descended on the Gustafsons' yellow colonial to clean and organize it, inside and out: lawn raked and mowed, weeds whacked and flowers planted, patio furniture cleaned and put away, back-door lock adjusted and rug washed, refrigerator cleaned out and clutter organized, Christmas decorations packed away and new plants put in their place. This was both a wonderful gift for Carole and a courageous act of surrender, accepting the help of friends.

I had been serving Townsend for nine months, far longer than the four months originally contracted. I had scheduled personal time, expecting to be on hiatus from interim ministry. I planned for coverage, while my heart broke because of the timing. I visited in Boston one last time, bringing communion, as well as also Tylenol, at Carole's request. This time we spoke about cherishing the time that remained and letting go into the arms of God. Andy had news for me. "God has let me know that I have done what I was called to do. I can let go now." We cried together.

Then Andy looked at me. "I am so blessed to have Carole in my life. She is so giving, so caring, so kind."

Turning to his wife, "I love you, Carole."

"I love you so much, Andy," she replied.

I arranged the communion set. I had visited the local priest to get dissolvable wafers especially for this day. I poured a drop or two of juice into the cup and served a small fraction of the wafer, wanting to provide an amount on which he would not choke. We remembered together the meaning of communion, the last meal with Jesus, the sharing of bread and cup through the ages. We prayed and ate together, feeling the Presence of Jesus near. After I finished serving the elements, Andy held out the cup. "I want more."

"Of course. There is abundance, more than we can ever imagine," I asserted, and filled the cup.

"It tastes so good," Andy relished.

"I can leave the bottle of juice."

"Could you?"

"All I have is yours."

We talked through how we would communicate in the next week and the plans for support that had been put in place. They were gracious and encouraging of my time away.

They had hoped to go home on Saturday, May 17; instead, it was Monday, May 19. Carole drove home alone while Andy came home by ambulance. Hospice organized his care, placing the hospital bed in the living room in much the same way that it had been done for Andy's mother. The care team administered more and more medication to manage the pain. Andy had less pain, and more time when he slept. Nevertheless, visitors came regularly.

Andy particularly wanted to see one of his long-time friends, to express again his deep appreciation for identifying the children that dreadful day. "I have never forgotten that act of courage you did on my behalf." They both cried. Andy talked individually with Laura and Holly, encouraging them, exchanging their deep love, wanting to give and receive everything that was possible.

The support people from hospice came and went regularly, providing the medicine to keep Andy as comfortable as possible, while Carole stayed by his side. By Wednesday night, only two days after he came home, Andy slipped into a coma. Sitting by his bedside, Carole prayed and cried. And then with conviction and clarity, she said aloud softly, "Go, my love, my best friend, my soul mate. Go back to your first family. Go back into the arms of Cilla, surrounded by the laughter and joy of Abby and Billy. I give you back to them." Carole dozed off and on in the chair at his bedside, touching him tenderly and shedding tears when she roused. The family gathered in the morning. The hospice nurse arrived with a shot to keep him comfortable.

Ellie, one of the conference ministers, texted, "Is there anything I can do?"

"No," came the initial response.

But a few minutes later, Carole called and said, "Yes. Come."

Within half an hour, Ellie arrived at the house in Townsend. Together, those gathered prayed and talked together. Ellie anointed Andy and said a beautiful, moving, sending prayer. They held hands and were present as Andy breathed his last breath. He passed away at 12:30 p.m. on Thursday, May 22, 2014.

People Remember

The conference announced Andy's death by email and a post on the website, drawing dozens of loving, heartfelt responses.

"Dear, sweet Andy. So humble and such a great encourager of others. My brother, hope you are free, and see face to face." - Molly Baskette

"Friend, Colleague, Counselor, Inspirational, Funny, Boss.... I am so sad at his long trial with Cancer to final passing. Andy and I had many meetings about churches that needed capital campaigns, and shared many joys with those churches when they succeeded, with the help of God. One church leader said, 'I felt the fingers of God throughout this whole process with us all. Welcome to a new Joy, Andy.'" Margarey Williams

"The former Executive Council of the now closed North Congregational Church, UCC of Amherst, MA, shares in the great sadness of all who are learning of Andy's passing. Without Andy's steadfast support, information, encouragement and genuine concern for our church and its members, we could not have brought the closing of North Church to a positive and meaningful conclusion.

He stood by us in our most difficult times and helped us know the true meaning of giving. Andy became part of North Church even as we prepared to turn the keys over to another faith group. We are thankful for the opportunity to get to know Andy and for his commitment to helping us through the final chapter of North Congregational Church, Amherst." - Barbara Jenkins and Faye Hollender

"I am overwhelmed with grief! He lived his faith out loud and I am grateful for all he taught me. He will be sorely missed. There is no doubt he is hearing the words today: Well Done My Good And Faithful Servant!" - Donna Spencer Collins

Carole and the family were showered with cards, notes, and visits. I had a previously set meeting on Saturday, with the family, intended for a visit with Andy. Instead, that Memorial Day weekend I met with Carole alone to grieve and to plan the funeral. I would preach the following day, and then the following weekend, the congregation would meet the proposed new pastor. Carole and I talked about options. She decided she would wait for a week until I returned two days after the presentation of the new pastor. She did not want to involve the funeral home very much and the extra time would allow her friends and family to organize the wake, the funeral, and the reception.

She and I conferred about the elements of the service, the people who would speak, the songs to sing, the choice of scriptures, the way to accommodate the choir. Carole seemed on top of almost everything, until there was a break in the flow of conversation. Carole almost froze and sat silently for a long time, staring upward and starting to tear up.

"What's happening?" I asked after a time of silence.

"What do I do with the ashes? Do I buy a stone for the two of us and bury them there? Do I bury them with Cilla and the kids? Do I not bury them at all? I don't know what to do, I feel so torn."

We sat in silence for a few moments.

"Maybe there is another way," I offered. "My son made the choice to divide the ashes of his wife. That way, her mother had some ashes to bury in Michigan, near them, and my son would have some to release on Mt. Monadnock."

Carole brightened. "That's something I've never thought of." She paused. "Actually, that feels amazing, freeing, in line with our life." She ordered two urns for the cemetery.

A week later, Andy's friends and family filled the church hallway and fellowship room with memorabilia, photographs, sporting awards, and a guest book. The communication specialist from the conference created a slide show of photographs and music. I walked into the hallway to see one table with a picture album of Cilla and their children, another with an album of Carole and their children, a Scrabble game with words capturing Andy's life laid out on a third table, and news clippings from West Brookfield and Townsend hung on a divider. And there was Flat Andy, perched ready to paddle the red solo kayak, sporting one of Andy's baseball caps. I smiled.

On Tuesday afternoon, church members stood outside to direct traffic, to invite people through the sanctuary doors, into the hallway, past the family's displays, and through the fellowship room to the family receiving area. When the reception began at four o'clock, fifty people waited to share their condolences. The line grew, stretching into the sanctuary at the peak. I moved around from the hallway where I hugged people who seemed to want that, or chatted with folks about their relationship with Andy, into the kitchen where I talked with family and enjoyed the food prepared by friends, into the fellowship hall where I sat in the circle of chairs around the slide show or brought refreshments to family members and church helpers who had been standing for a long time. Fellow clergy who were particularly touched by Andy told stories, townspeople who had known Andy for decades paid their respects, church members grieved his loss, cousins recalled memories at family reunions.

One young woman whom I had never met reached out for a hug as she began to cry. "I took care of Abby and Billy. All that comes streaming back to me. It was so terrible."

A church member confided, "Andy was the person who made me feel at home in the church. We talked about the Bible many times. He made faith come alive for me."

A fellow clergyperson greeted me. "Andy's parents were part of my congregation. They were salt of the earth, and Andy loved them so much."

Family members and close friends in the kitchen noted, "Andy would really have liked that soup, and eaten half of the sandwiches on that platter."

The flow of people continued for more than four hours. As we neared nine o'clock, the end of calling hours, everyone had been greeted, additional church members appeared to clean up, and Carole took the lead to design the altar area for the funeral the next day. I packed up for my hour's drive home, exhausted. Finally, Carole left too, leaving others to complete the finishing touches in the sanctuary and in the hall for the reception the next day.

The Celebration of a Life Well Lived

The funeral day was overcast, with intermittent rain. The yellow colonial buzzed with people. Hunter barked as I knocked. Laura held his collar as Carole open the door. "Hunter, it's just Betsy. Relax. Laura, can you put him behind the gate?"

As I turned, Carole offered, "Would you like some food? We have so much."

"Maybe a little fruit," I replied, as I took a few pieces from the platter.

"I'm worried about Peter Wells. I heard from folks in the conference that he is flying in from Iowa and there are tornados in the area," Carole noted anxiously.

"We'll figure it out," I comforted. "I just trust he will be safe."

"Let me introduce you to my family." Carole took me into the living room to meet a few people, but then got distracted by a voice calling her from the kitchen. Her brother, a small, white-haired gentleman from Tennessee, adopted me, introducing me to the rest of the family, finding an umbrella for me, and providing a ride to the cemetery and back. He confided that he needed to leave promptly because he had postponed his own chemo treatment in order to come.

We had scheduled the funeral for four o'clock to accommodate the choir. A private gathering at the cemetery preceded the funeral

service. About two dozen gathered in the drizzle, near the rear of
the cemetery, with the stone for Cilla and the children in one row
and Greg's stone in the next row, two or three plots away. There
was a small table with two urns and a bouquet of red roses. The
group encircled both stones, some in raincoats, some under um-
brellas, some receiving the drips of rain on their head. Laura held
two year old Avari, some older children and teens huddled next to
their parents, many couples held hands.

"Do not let your hearts be troubled. Believe in God, believe
also in me..." I began. The group took an audible breath.

We prayed, we listened to scripture, we acknowledged the
stones around which we stood.

I invited the group to offer a few words of description, of connection, of remembrance of Andy. The words came from different
places around the circle: "father," "friend," "courageous soul," "husband," "spiritual leader," "brother."

"You were my best friend, Dad, a wonderful grandfather," Laura offered almost inaudibly.

"I love you..." whispered several in the circle.

The words gradually diminished and the group came to still-
ness, listening to the raindrops.

"Into your hands, O merciful Savior, we commend your servant Andrew Gustafson. Acknowledge, we humbly pray, a sheep
of your own fold, a lamb of your own flock, a son of your own re-
deeming. Receive him into the arms of your mercy, into the blessed rest of everlasting peace, and into the company of the saints in
Light."

I took a long breath.

"You are invited to take one of these roses and place it in memory."

Carole took Avari's hand and walked with her to place two
roses, one on each urn. Avari stood quietly for a moment, and
then ran over to her mother, calling softly.

As people finished their time of remembrance and prayer, they gathered under the tree with spreading branches and new leaves budding. At first the people just looked down at the ground, and then in a few moments they looked at each other, or chatted quietly.

"What shall we do now? There is almost two hours to the service," one voice asked.

"How about ice cream?" someone suggested. "An ice cream for Andy, just like he would do at Howard's Drive-In, back in his home town of West Brookfield."

Yes, everyone agreed.

"Where do we find that?"

"Bear left at the intersection. Swing round the common to the stoplight. Immediately after the light, there is a stand on the right."

They piled into different cars to buy ice cream while Carole's brother drove me back to the house and I returned to church to make final preparations.

A little more than an hour later, the street around the common filled with cars, the organ began the prelude, and people walked across the common on their way to the church. The sanctuary filled up quickly with a wide range of people. In the center was a simple altar with a cross, a picture of Andy, and flower bouquets labeled husband, father, brother. I stopped to greet people from the conference and to check in with the ushers.

The family gathered in the sitting room behind the sanctuary, spilling over into the hall, talking together, checking cell phones, and finding the baby sitter who would care for Avari and one of the cousins. A member of the conference staff notified us that Peter Wells had arrived safely, bringing some relief.

"Do we have someone who might want to light the candles?" I asked.

Niece Hailey was suggested. "But she's not here. She's over at the house. I'll call," offered Carole. With that, plans were made. We checked to see who was missing. In just a few minutes, the last of the family arrived.

I invited the group to make a circle. "Let us be in the spirit of prayer." The family held hands, became quiet, prayed, and prepared to enter the sanctuary. Without funeral parlor support, one of the church members organized the procession and I led the family into the church, the family on my left, and the conference staff on my right.

Once the candles had been lit and the organist finished the prelude, the sanctuary became silent. The church clock chimed almost as if it were synchronized with our actions. Cilla's two sisters and brothers came forward to the piano to sing as they had sung in this place twice before. For ears to hear, their song echoed Cilla's and Abby's sweet voices heard here so many years ago. Tears flowed.

I stood. "The peace of Christ be with you."

The congregation responded, "And also with you."

This day, I really needed those words. Off and on through the service, my eyes filled with tears. The congregation stood to affirm their faith, singing together one of Andy's favorite hymns, "Be Thou My Vision."

"Friends," I continued, "we gather here in the protective shelter of God's healing love. We are free to pour out our grief, release our anger, face our emptiness, and know that God cares."

"We remember Andy, a humble man of profound faith, who shared laughter wherever he went, who was a beacon of God's Light and love in the world. A husband, father, grandfather, brother, leader, teacher, friend, preacher with conviction, a faithful steward, a lawyer and advocate for children, a cross-country skier and kayaker, a fan of the Red Sox and of camping on the Saco, and one who loved to sing—and tried quite loudly, actually, but he wasn't so good at that."

The whole room erupted in knowing laughter.

We prayed together, listened to scripture from Luke, Psalms, and Second Corinthians, and the choir sang. Then a parade of people came to offer remembrances. Brother Larry came with his daughter Judy to speak of their lifetime bond. Cilla's three siblings recalled Andy and their sister's courtship and their life with Abby and Billy. Two friends described fun times and the challenge of the years following the murders. Peter Wells filled the space with his swinging arms and a booming voice, his own laughter covering his deep grief. Holly and Laura witnessed to the love and respect they knew from their father.

Somewhat unscripted, Carole made her way up front. "I had to come. I had to tell you how much I love him, how much I miss him, how much I admire him, how hard he fought." I hugged Carole before she returned to her seat and signaled the organist to lead us in "Angels We have Heard on High."

The conference president, the Rev. Jim Antal, came forward to lead prayer. He captured what we all were feeling.

"Gracious God," he began, "who are we that you should grant us the opportunity to serve alongside such goodness? Surrounded as we are by unceasing opportunities for compromise, tempted as we are to be judgmental or to lose hope, you bless us by providing a friend whose moral purity invited us to soar, to be strong and resilient, to allow joy to infect and convert our most sorrowful places. As often as we were completely overcome by Andy's laughter, let us honor his memory by bringing joy to others. As often as we were moved by his wisdom or freed by his insight, let us honor his memory by bringing our 'best selves' to every challenge we are given. As often as we experience the world as ruled by scarcity, let us honor Andy's memory by invoking the abundance you continuously renew. Turn us, we pray, from grief to gratitude for the blessing of having known your servant Andy, and the opportunity you give us today—and every day——to join Andy in witnessing to your kingdom. Thank you for giving us one who testified to your promise that your kingdom is here—your kingdom is now—and you are in our midst."

A week or two later, Jim Antal sent out a message to the whole conference announcing a time in honor of Andy Gustafson, "to remember and share the lessons of faith, generosity and making God's love and justice real" at the Annual Meeting in early June. So, on Saturday afternoon of the annual gathering, the room filled with extra guests. Cilla's sisters joined Carole, a couple of the conference staff and me at a front table. Conference staff, with slides showing pictures of Andy paired with key themes flashing behind the podium, led the group in sharing stories about what he taught, stories that continue his legacy. Carole spoke of her love and respect for Andy, mentioning the murders of his first family, assuming that it was common knowledge. The audible gasp made it clear that many people there had not known that part of Andy's history. That is when I first felt God raising questions in me. Do more people need to know Andy's story? Was that a piece of Andy's feeling his work was not done? Is this something that I am called to do? I think the seeds of this project were planted then.

At the usual time for camping, Carole joined Larry, the family, and some close friends at the Saco River. She brought with her a small container of ashes. Larry paddled out into the middle of the flowing river and scattered some. They sprinkled some near the fire. They said a prayer and sang a song. A few months later, Carole was again by the Saco, coffee in hand, early in the morning. A blue heron landed very near her, lingering a long time. Carole knew, somehow, that Andy had visited her. Andy was her angel now.

As for me, Andy has been imprinted on my heart in more ways than I understand. One of the best ways to express this is to quote a blog post Andy wrote on creating an annual stewardship campaign linked to a church's ministry.

> "...telling your story of how in the past year you have changed lives, how your corner of the world is better because of what you have done in the name of Jesus Christ. There is Good News to proclaim: the Gospel has been proclaimed to your young and old alike, the hungry have been fed, the lonely have been visited, the sick have been prayed over and have been wrapped in prayer shawls and love, justice has been sought, the poor in far off lands have received clean water, the alienated have been welcomed into fellowship, and the despairing have been given new hope. The reign of God is truly visible in our midst because of your ministries in this past year. Proclaim it!"[12]

And so, I began to research and write this story.

Appendices

Small Group Study Guides

What follows are three different study guides for small groups:
1) The Spiritual Journey
2) The Journey of Grief and Resurrection
3) Topic focused Reflections on Andy's Life and Our Lives.

Each group will meet six to eight times. These guides are designed to be flexible and use open-ended questions that can be adapted to different time frames, levels of intimate sharing, and theological perspectives. Topic focused reflection groups are the easiest to offer as a "drop-in" model where people come to only some of the gatherings. Each session includes some questions focused on Andy's life, and some on the participants' lives. In addition, inviting people to share thoughts that have stirred between sessions or questions they have been pondering will build continuity and depth.

Although not required, a group facilitator who establishes norms of respectful listening, highlights and clarifies useful language, and adapts to the needs of the people involved is very helpful. Some leaders can assist groups in creating their own norms, adding things from the suggested list below. Others would prefer to be given a set of norms.

Suggested Norms

1. Practice respect, including: tone of voice, use of language, and body language.

2. Listen actively, without interruption or holding side conversations.

3. Take turns, giving everyone about the same amount of time to talk.

4. The goal is deeper understanding, not convincing others of your opinion. Listening does not imply agreement, and disagreement does not require contradicting the speaker.

5. Particularly when considering Andy's life, clarifying, curious questions can build mutual understanding of how people use language.

6. Appreciate the insights of others, while speaking for yourself.

Theme Series:
The Spiritual Journey

Session 1: The Apocalypse

What was Andy's apocalypse? What expectations were broken? What changed?

Share a major blow in your life or in the life of someone you love. What expectations were broken? What changed?

Who else was affected and how?

Who else was affected and how?

If you are able, identify some of the apocalyptic scripture.

How do you interpret those scriptures in light of these events?

Session 2: Support, Pastoral Care

Who supported Andy, and how?

Who supported you, and how?

In what ways were Andy's support people unable to help? Why?

In what ways were your support people unable to help? Why?

Session 3: Spiritual Practice

What kind of spiritual practices had Andy learned earlier in his life that helped in this crisis?

What kind of spiritual practices had you learned that helped you in this crisis?
What was missing?

Knowing what you know, what might the church teach to prepare people for tragedy in their lives?

Session 4: Values and Insights

What were some of the insights and larger perspectives that Andy gained as part of his healing journey, or Carole's?

What were some of the insights and larger perspectives that you gained as part of your healing journey?

What values were realigned in his recovery?

What values were realigned in your recovery?

Session 5: Shaping New Life Choices

How did Andy live differently in the years following his grief journey? How did this experience affect his choices around money, purpose, and work?

How have you lived differently as a result of reflecting on your life challenges? How has this experience affected your choices around money, purpose, and work?

Session 6: Authenticity and Humor

Most people described Andy as an authentic, spirit-filled man. He could laugh and cry, express doubts and convictions, ask different questions, and create commotion. How did you respond to Andy as a person?

Is authenticity a value or goal for you? Why or why not? How does humor function in your life? Are you joyful? Is that a value or goal for you? How does creativity enter your life?

Theme Series: The Grief Journey

Session 1: Telling the Story of Grief (may take two sessions)

The book began with the murders of Andy's family, but then unwrapped the joy of their life together. The tragedy and the love are mixed together, amplifying the loss. Telling the story is important.

Share your story of grief—the loss and the love, the joy and the sorrow, the things that went well, and the parts of your life that were less than stellar.

Session 2: A Listening Presence

Carole listened to Andy with much patience, giving him space to feel his feelings, to express his fears, to ask his questions. She was his witness without trying to change him. Highlight some examples from the book that caught your attention.

Who has been there for you in your grief journey? What has been most helpful? What has interfered or led you to shut down? Are there thoughts about that journey you have not shared and would like to? Are there things you would ask from this group?

Recall the grief group's meeting plan.

Would that be helpful here? If so, how?

Session 3: Setting goals

Andy set goals for himself to help with the healing. What do you think of his process and his goals? What do you think of his decision to remarry? To adopt? What things helped him move forward?

What goals did you set for yourself? What might you set for yourself? Where are you stuck? What would more letting-go look like for you? What interferes with letting go more? What encourages it?

Session 4: Residual Effects of Grief

Andy continued to have emotional turmoil, particularly at night, for years after the event, although the intensity of it decreased. Name some tools and resources he used to help him, both spiritual and practical. What memorials were helpful?

Where are you today on your grief journey? Are you aware of continued grieving? What are some of the tools and resources you have used, both spiritual and practical? What memorials might be helpful?

How did Andy wrestle with death as the "intolerable mystery"?

How do you wrestle with death as the "intolerable mystery"?

Session 5: Forgiveness

Andy took some steps toward forgiving LaPlante, and some steps were more than he could take. Review and discuss Andy's journey of forgiveness.

What kind of forgiveness work have you done? What is left undone?

Session 6 – Choices

Andy initially thought he would not treat the cancer, and then changed his mind. He also wrestled with choices near the end of his treatment cycle. What influenced his choices? Consider history, relationships, and faith convictions.

How have you dealt with such medical issues in your life? What would your goals be? What influences your choices. Consider your history, relationships, and faith convictions.

Theme Series:
Topic focused Reflections on Andy's Life and Our Lives.

Session 1: Violence, Tragedy, and Evil

Identify some of the places in the book that refer to violence and tragedy.

Do you equate violence to evil? How do you make sense of a world where there is so much violence and tragedy? How would you talk about evil? About sin?

Andy was clear that he did not believe that God caused these murders, and that God was crying with him. What do you understand that Andy believed about God's power?

Where is God for you in this story? What do you think about Andy's experience of God crying with him? Does that matter? What do you believe about God's power and violence/evil?

Session 2: Love, Compassion and Caring

Who showed Andy love, compassion, and caring and how did they do it?

What have you experienced as love, compassion, and caring from others?

When have you offered love, compassion, and caring? How was it received?

Session 3: Experiencing God's Presence: Prayer and Spiritual Practice

How did Andy experience God over his lifetime? In what settings, under what conditions, with what questions?

How have you experienced God over your lifetime? In what settings, under what conditions, with what questions?

A spiritual practice can be defined as an intentional activity, usually done repeatedly, that brings us closer to God and nourishes or deepens that relationship with the Holy. Spiritual practices can be done alone or with others. What spiritual practices do you recognize in Andy's life? Consider worship, prayer, gratitude, and solitude, among others.

In what spiritual practices have you engaged? How have they sustained you? What might you do to make them stronger?

Session 4: Money

Andy had difficulty balancing his family budget, but was exceedingly generous with the church. How do you understand the thought process that led him to give so freely?

What are your thoughts about money and generosity? What guides your decisions and priorities? What questions do you ask? To whom do you listen? How do hopes and fears impact those choices?

Andy could talk joyfully about generosity and giving. Find an example to read aloud.

Discuss your feelings about asking for money for churches/good causes. How do you feel about having people ask you for money? What motivates your generosity? What inhibits your giving?

Session 5: Transforming Lives

Andy recognized that the church had changed his life. He gained purpose and meaning by doing things that could positively impact other people. How?

What is your life purpose? Is any part of it connected to transforming the lives of others? How do you imagine that happening?

Andy told of having a community work together to build a Habitat House and the positive ripples from that. (p. 147-49)

Have you participated in a mission project that had that kind of ripple effect?

Session 6: The Church

Andy loved the church. Find some quotes and descriptions that capture Andy's concept of church: its purpose, its gift and its story. (Some possibilities: p. 51, 190, 217)

In what ways does church matter to you? What do you find frustrating or problematic for you about church? What would make it better?

A Stewardship Campaign:
Testify to the Light

Andy equipped churches and church leaders to inspire generosity. He continues to do so through a wealth of resources posted through the portal at www.macucc.org/stewardship. A team planning a stewardship campaign is encouraged to access these resources. In addition, Andy was active in supporting many other resource-sharing groups, including the Northeast Ecumenical Stewardship Council (nestewardship.org) and the School of Philanthropy at Indiana University.

What is presented in this section assumes a basic understanding of how an annual campaign is organized. Instead, this section offers a theme for one campaign inspired by the story of Andy's life. It includes possible scriptures and conversation starters for worship planning, for small group discussions, an all-church conversation event at which stewardship materials would be distributed, and a culminating worship focused on testimony. This is created with this book in mind. It likely could be adapted for other similarly inspiring faith stories.

Six to twelve months before the campaign, the stewardship leadership reads and discusses the book, using this experience to introduce Andy's story and the campaign. Then, the stewards invite leaders of Adult Christian Formation to read the book in advance and to organize one or more book discussion series two months before the all-church stewardship event.

Suggested Scriptures

John 8:12-15
John 1: 7-8
John 1: 4-5
Matthew 5: 15-16

General Resources on Testimony

Preaching as Testimony, Anna Carter Florence
Testimony, Talking Ourselves into Being Christian, Tom Long
Tell it Like it Is: Reclaiming the Practice of Testimony, Lillian Daniels

All Church Stewardship Event (2-3 hours, depending on the length of eating)

Preparation for Church Stewardship Event

Plan a nourishing snack or simple meal, such as cheese, crackers and veggies or soup and sandwiches. A longer version could include a potluck or catered meal. The goal is to have minimal kitchen work needed during this event.

Prepare written stewardship materials in advance, putting people's names on the envelopes so that those who do not attend can be mailed the materials. This material includes some kind of narrative budget, an appeal letter, a pledge card, and an invitation to the stewardship celebration worship.

For the all-church event, set the room up, with chairs in clusters of three or four in a circle around a room. Be sure the leader in the room can be heard, providing amplification if needed. Each of the clusters has at least one person who has read the book and who has a copy of the questions. That person does not move from his or her seat. The other members of the circle get a direction card instructing them how to move around the circle. The cards read: Clockwise, Counter-clockwise, and Random (this person could stay put, if there are mobility limitations). Provide arrows on the floor to indicate clockwise and counter clockwise directions. Provide name-tags for every person.

People do not need to have read the book to participate in this event. It is a great opportunity to meet new people, to build community, to mix people who have been in the church for years with those who are relatively new.

Recruit a Master of Ceremonies, a kitchen leader, a welcome team, and a team to distribute the written materials.

The Event

Invite people to sit in clusters of three or four. Adjust numbers to fit the people who come, starting with three in each group and adding the fourth as extra people appear. Explain that group conversations will last 10-15 minutes each. With each new question, people move to their next group. At the beginning of each question, make sure everyone has been introduced in your group.

Round 1:
What do you know about Andy Gustafson's story? What do you find inspiring in it and why? What questions do you have?

Round 2:
Andy's church and community were a great support following the murders of his wife and children. How has this church been a community of support in times of grief, struggle or hardship?

How has this touched your life?

Round 3:

Andy's church took a risk—setting a high goal during their capital campaign to fund a Habitat house and ended up engaging the whole town in the building. (Reference: pp. 147-49) This section ends with this quote...

And all it took was generosity, the generosity of time, talent, and treasure. Andy had told them this in the abstract, but now they had seen this with their own eyes, had helped with their own hands, had shared out of their own pockets, and had experienced the joy spread throughout the community.

Have you ever had this kind of experience? Share your stories.

Round 4:

Andy's relationship with money changed over the course of his life, from wanting to make a million dollars, to choosing to give generously, and to willingly sharing his story and asking others to give. (pp. 64-5, 141-42, 160)

What do you think allowed that to happened and why? How do you feel about it?

Where are you on your journey with money? How has the church influenced that journey?

** Take a break to eat together. Distribute materials now

Round 5:

"What we do as a church, it's important," Andy preached. "What we do is important to the people here, to the town, to the children, to the children not yet born. What we do here is nourish the Light, the Light that is proclaimed on that cemetery stone just over that hill," Andy gestured broadly. "We shine God's Light, the Light that shines in the darkness, together. We must. It matters. What we do matters to the world." (p. 180)

Why does your church matter—to you, to the people here, to your community, to the children, to the children not yet born?

Completing the Event

Gather people into a circle. Give thanks for people's participation and help, and for the distribution of stewardship materials. Announce the celebration worship (with dedication of pledge cards). Close with prayer and/or singing (maybe This Little Light of Mine or something similar).

The Celebration Worship Service

Consider using Andy's words in preparation and during the service.

"...telling your story of how in the past year you have changed lives, how your corner of the world is better because of what you have done in the name of Jesus Christ. There is Good News to proclaim: the gospel has been proclaimed to your young and old alike, the hungry have been fed, the lonely have been visited, the sick have been prayed over and have been wrapped in prayer shawls and love, justice has been strived for, the poor in far off lands have received clean water, the alienated have been welcomed into fellowship, and the despairing have been given new hope. The reign of God is truly visible in our midst because of your ministries in this past year. Proclaim it!"

Invite both planned and spontaneous testimony during the celebration worship, perhaps using the John 1:7-8 text, having people testify to the Light they have seen, God with us, in skin.

Endnotes

1. Diego Ribadeneira and Doris Sue Wong, Globe Staff. "Police Seeking 17-Year-Old Suspect of Three in Townsend" The Boston Globe (Boston, MA). *The New York Times* Company. 1987. *HighBeam Research.* 31 Aug. 2015 <http://www.highbeam.com>.

2. Paul Langner, Globe Staff. "Trooper: LaPlante Said He Heard of Deaths on TV; Investigator Says Murder Trial Defendant Told Him He Spent Most of That Day at Home." The Boston Globe (Boston, MA) *The New York Times* Company 1988. *HighBeam Research.* 30 Aug. 2015 <http://www.highbeam.com>

3. Peter J. Howe, Globe Staff. "In Townsend, Comfort Amid the Tears: Family's Sole Survivor Leads 400 Mourners at Funeral of 3 Murder Victims." The *Boston Globe* (Boston, MA) The New York Times Company 1988. *HighBeam Research.* 31 Aug. 2015 <http://www.highbeam.com>

4. Andy Gustafson, quoted by Bella English, Globe Staff. "As Trial Begins, A Father Remembers His Slain Family." The *Boston Globe* (Boston, MA) The New York Times Company 1988. *HighBeam Research.* 30 Aug. 2015 <http://www.highbeam.com>

5. Paul Langner, Globe Staff. "Judge Releases Impounded Jail Letters." The Boston Globe (Boston, MA) *The New York Times* Company 1988. *HighBeam Research.* 30 Aug. 2015 <http://www.highbeam.com>

6. Paul Langner, Globe Staff. "Judge in LaPlante Murder Case Rules Youth Must Be Tried on 4 Charges." The Boston Globe (Boston, MA) *The New York Times* Company 1988. *HighBeam Research.* 30 Aug. 2015 <http://www.highbeam.com>

7. AP, "Jurors are Selected for LaPlante Trial," The Boston Globe (Boston, MA). The New York Time Company. 1988. High Beam Research. 30 Aug. 2015 <http://www.highbeam.com>

8. Paul Langner, Globe Staff. "LaPlante Jury Hears Girl, 9, Recall Screams." The Boston Globe (Boston, MA) *The New York Times* Company 1988. *HighBeam Research.* 30 Aug. 2015 <http://www.highbeam.com>

9. Paul Langner, Globe Staff. "Gustafson Cries as He Testifies about Finding His Wife's Body." The Boston Globe (Boston, MA) *The New York Times* Company 1988. *HighBeam Research.* 30 Aug. 2015 <http://www.highbeam.com>

10. Paul Langner, Globe Staff. "LaPlante Convicted, Gets Life in 3 Killings." The *Boston Globe* (Boston, MA) The New York Times Company 1988. *HighBeam Research.* 30 Aug. 2015 <http://www.highbeam.com>

11. Andy Gustafson, "The Substance of Our Faith." Massachusetts Conference United Church of Christ. 31 Aug. 2015. <http://www.macucc.org/blogdetail/93067>

12. Andy Gustafson, "The Great Annual Meeting Opportunity." Massachusetts Conference United Church of Christ. 31 Aug 2015 <http://www.macucc.org/blogdetail/93212>

Bibliography

Cullens, Kevin; Kindleberger, Richard; Langer, Paul; Lewis, Diane E.; Ribadeneira, Diego and Wond, Doris Sue. "A Youth Who Sowed Fear." *Boston Globe* (Boston, MA) 1987. *High Beam Research*. 31 Aug. 2015 <http://www.highbeam.com>

Cullen, Kevin; Ribadeneira, Diego, and Wong, Doris Sue, Globe Staff. "Suspect is Captured in Slayings." The *Boston Globe* (Boston, MA) 1987. *HighBeam Research*. 31 Aug. 2015 <http://www.highbeam.com>

Gustafson, Andrew, "Changing Lives Tour." Massachusetts Conference United Church of Christ. 31 Aug. 2015 <macucc.org>

Gustafson, Andrew, "The Substance of Our Faith." Massachusetts Conference United Church of Christ. 31 Aug. 2015 <macucc.org>

Howe, Peter, "In Townsend, Comfort Amid the Tears: Family's Sole Survivor Leads 400 Mourners at the Funeral of the 3 Murder Victims." *Boston Globe* (Boston, MA) *HighBeam Research*. 31 Aug. 2015 <http://www.highbeam.com>

Kennedy, Dana, Associated Press. "Man Who Found Slain

Family Learns to Rebuild His Life From Tragedy." 1990 *Los Angeles Times* (Los Angeles, CA) 31 Aug. 2015 <http://www.articles.latimes.com>

Langner, Paul, Globe Staff. "Gustafson Cries as He Testifies about Finding His Wife's Body." The *Boston Globe* (Boston, MA) Oct 9, 1988. *HighBeam Research*. 31 Aug. 2015 <http://www.highbeam.com>

Langner, Paul, Globe Staff. "LaPlante Had Capable Defense in Murder Trial, Lawyers Say." The *Boston Globe* (Boston, MA) The New York Times Company 1988. *HighBeam Research*. 31 Aug. 2015 <http://www.highbeam.com>

Langner, Paul, Globe Staff. "LaPlante Convicted, Gets Life in 3 Killings." The Boston Globe (Boston, MA) The *New York Times* Company 1988. *HighBeam Research*. 31 Aug. 2015 <http://www.highbeam.com>

Langner, Paul, Globe Staff. "LaPlante's Stepfather Says He Found Revolver." The *Boston Globe* (Boston, MA) The New York Times Company 1988. *HighBeam Research*. 31 Aug. 2015 <http://www.highbeam.com>

Langner, Paul, Globe Staff. "LaPlante's Mother Contradictory When Testifying about Evidence." The *Boston Globe* (Boston, MA) The New York Times Company 1988. *HighBeam Research*. 31 Aug. 2015 <http://www.highbeam.com>.

Langner, Paul, Globe Staff. "LaPlante Murder Trial Lawyers Rest Their Cases." The *Boston Globe* (Boston, MA) The New York Times Company 1988. *HighBeam Research*. 31 Aug. 2015 <http://www.highbeam.com>

Langner, Paul, Globe Staff. "Man Testifies He Sold Bullets to LaPlante Before Killings." The *Boston Globe* (Boston, MA) The New York Times Company 1988. *HighBeam Research.* 31 Aug. 2015 <http://www.highbeam.com>

Langner, Paul, Globe Staff. "Trooper Describes Steps in Capture of Suspect in Townsend Killings." The *Boston Globe* (Boston, MA) The *New York Times* Company 1988. *HighBeam Research.* 31 Aug. 2015 <http://www.highbeam.com>

Langner, Paul, Globe Staff. "Trooper: LaPlante said He Heard of Deaths on TV; Investigator Says Murder Trial Defendant Told Him He Spent Most of That Day at Home." The *Boston Globe* (Boston, MA) The New York Times Company 1988. *HighBeam Research.* 31 Aug. 2015 <http://www.highbeam.com>

Langner, Paul, Globe Staff. "Trooper Links Revolver to Townsend Killings: Ballistics Specialist Says Bullet Casings Found at Scene Were Fired from Stolen Pistol." The *Boston Globe* (Boston, MA) The *New York Times* Company 1988. *HighBeam Research.* 31 Aug. 2015 <http://www.highbeam.com>

Langner, Paul, Globe Staff. "Scene of Townsend Slaying Described at Trial." The *Boston Globe* (Boston, MA) The New York Times Company 1988. *HighBeam Research.* 31 Aug. 2015 <http://www.highbeam.com>

Langner, Paul, Globe Staff. "Witness Describes Abduction by LaPlante." The *Boston Globe* (Boston, MA) The New York Times Company 1988. *HighBeam Research.* 31 Aug. 2015 <http://www.highbeam.com>

LAPLANTE, COMMONWEALTH vs. 416 Mass. 433 (LAPLANTE, COMMONWEATH vs., 416 Mass. 433) http://masscases.com/cases/sjc/416/416mass433.html

May, William. *Once Upon a Crisis: A Look at Post-Traumatic Stress in Emergency Services from the Inside Out.* Mindstir Media, 2012. Print.

Minch, Jack, "Past Always Present in Gustafson's Life," Sentinel and Enterprise, Fitchburg, Ma. 2007. <http://www.sentinelandenterprise.com/mobile/ci_7623450>

Ribadeneira, Diego and Wong, Doris Sue, Globe Staff. "Police Seeking 17-Year-Old Suspect for Slayings of Three in Townsend." The *Boston Globe* (Boston, MA) The New York Times Company 1988. *HighBeam Research.* 31 Aug. 2015 <http://www.highbeam.com>

Vail, Tiffany, communication specialist, compiler, "Sad News-- our beloved brother in Christ, Andy has died." Massachusetts Conference United Church of Christ. 31 Aug. 2015 <macucc.org>

Vail, Tiffany, communication specialist, compiler, "Inspiring Generosity (Stewardship)." Massachusetts Conference United Church of Christ. 31 Aug. 2015 <macucc.org>

About the Author

M. Elizabeth Waters, often called Betsy, is an intentional interim minister in the United Church of Christ and a Parish Consultant in the United Methodist Church. Her work as a passionate advocate of organizational transformation begins with deepening the spiritual practices of individuals within the congregation. Trained in educational psychology, teaching, organizational development, parish ministry and preaching, she is a creative learner open to the wonder of this world.

Made in the USA
Middletown, DE
05 February 2016